easy to grow!
Vegetables

Good Housekeeping

easy to grow!
Vegetables

COLLINS & BROWN

First published in the United Kingdom in 2010 by
Collins & Brown
10 Southcombe Street
London
W14 0RA

An imprint of Anova Books Company Ltd

The Good Housekeeping website is
www.allboutyou.com/goodhousekeeping

10 9 8 7 6 5 4 3 2 1

ISBN 978-1-84340-538-2
A catalogue record for this book is available from
the British Library.

Reproduction by Dot Gradations Ltd, UK
Printed and bound by Times Offset, Malaysia

This book can be ordered direct from the publisher at
www.anovabooks.com

The following pictures are reproduced with kind permission of GAP
picture library and Dave Bevan, Juliette Wade, Jonathan Buckley,
Clive Nichols, Howard Rice, JS Sira, Marcus Harpur, Maxine Adcock,
Elke Borkowski, Jerry Harpur, FhF Greenmedia, Fiona McLeod, Geoff
Kidd, Keith Burdett, Rob Whitworth and Jo Whitworth:
P.10; P.11; P.16; P.19; P.30; P.33; P.40; P.42; P.52; P.56; P.78;
P.82; P.83; P.96; P.99; P.100; P.108; P.110; P.119; P.125;
P.127 (R).

Line illustration on page 29 drawn by Trina Dalziel.

Colour photography by Lucinda Symons on the following pages:
P.20 (L,R); P.21 (L,R); P.22 (L,R); P.23 (L,R); P.24 (L,R); P.25 (L,R);
P.26 (L,R); P.27 (L,R); P.36 (R); P.37; P.38 (L,R).

The Publisher would like to thank Ginkgo Gardens for the kind use
of their centre

Contents

Basics

Tools and materials

Before you get started on your vegetable garden, you are going to need a basic set of tools. Always buy the best you can afford. Saving money on tools is a false economy. Choose those made from stainless steel with solid wood handles. Never buy unseen – try them out for size and comfort first.

It will make a big difference to your workload if your tools are comfortable to use. Take good care of them, as well. Clean off mud and soil after use and wipe them over with a cloth before putting them away. Service them regularly and sharpen them as necessary and they will last you for years.

Basic set

Spade: An essential tool, needed for heavy digging, breaking up clods, moving soil. They come in many different sizes and shapes, which is why you need to try them to find the one that suits you best. Make sure that the tread on the shoulders fits your foot comfortably, as well.

Fork: Used for loosening soil and breaking it down, especially after digging, and for lifting plants. The prongs are either round or flat – though if you are only buying one, the latter may be more useful, as they do the minimum of damage to tubers when lifting potatoes and other roots.

Rake: Used for levelling soil, preparing seedbeds, removing stones and debris. Widths vary, but an 8 to 10-tooth rake is adequate for most purposes. It is very important to make sure the weight and balance are right for you, as it is difficult to work with one that is too heavy or cumbersome.

Hoe: You will need two types: the Dutch hoe, which has a flat rectangular blade that is used, as you walk backwards, to remove weeds, loosen soil or draw a drill; and the draw or swan-necked hoe, which has a blade at right angles to the handle. This is pulled towards you rather than pushed away, and is useful on heavier soils and for earthing up.

Hand trowel and fork: The trowel is a versatile tool, but is primarily used for planting. The fork is useful for weeding near plants and loosening soil. They need to be sturdy and well made. They come in different shapes and sizes, so take your time to find the one that is most comfortable for you.

Garden line: Essential for making sure your rows are straight when planting seeds. You can buy them, or make your own by tying twine to two short canes.

Cultivator: Not essential, but the three to five claw-like prongs are useful for breaking up ground and weeding between plants.

Mattock: This is a heavy chisel-bladed hoe, again not essential, but sometimes easier to use on hard ground.

Pocket knife: Invaluable for slitting open bags of compost or manure, cutting twine, taking cuttings, etc.

Sharpening stone: Useful to have to keep edges sharp and well maintained.

Secateurs/shears: For pruning, cutting, keeping things tidy.

Others

Watering can: Chose a sturdy one – plastic or metal – with a capacity of seven to nine litres (1½–2 gallons). You will need two detachable roses – one coarse and one fine – so you can match flow to plant.

Wheelbarrow: For moving large amounts of soil, manure, plants, bags and so on. Again, size and balance is personal and you may find a secondhand one does the job as well.

Bucket: For holding soil and liquid materials, or moving quantities of stuff around the plot.

Carrying sheet or bag: Keep nearby while working

Hand tools
Good quality hand tools with solid wood handles will last longer and make gardening much easier.

to save time on trips to the compost heap or shed.

Bamboo canes: A selection of various sizes for marking out areas or positions, and providing support for plants, nets and wire.

Twine: For tying up branches, stems, canes, wires, etc.

Gloves: Choose a lighter, supple pair for pruning and planting, and a heavy duty pair for messier jobs such as handling prickly and stinging plants.

Horticultural fleece: To protect plants from the cold or pests, or to warm up the ground.

Cloches: A variety of different shapes, sizes and materials, including glass, plastic and polyurethane. For covering rows or individual plants – useful if you want to bring forward or extend the growing season, or for warming up the soil prior to sowing or planting.

Cold frames: Used for bringing on young plants or protecting a growing crop. They can be static with a solid floor, or movable (without a floor) to offer protection for plants growing in the ground, or adapted to make a hot bed.

For sowing seeds

Seed trays and small pots: Made of plastic (though wooden and terracotta types are also available) and

used for sowing seeds that need to be pricked out when they have germinated.

Modules: For sowing individual seeds to grow on to the planting out stage.

Biodegradable pots: Used for sowing crops that do not like their roots disturbed. Once the seedling is large enough to be planted out in the ground, the whole thing can go in and the container will rot down as the plant grows.

Dibber: A pointed metal or wood tool used to make holes for planting seeds or young plants. A small one is used for pricking out seedlings.

Labels and markers: Essential so you know what is where. Many different types are available in plastic, wood or slate with an appropriate pencil or pen.

Propagator lids: Usually made of clear plastic and put over seed trays to speed up germination. You could also use cut-off plastic bottles set over individual pots.

Electric propagator: A small unit in which seeds are placed when a specific temperature is needed to germinate them (usually 13–16°C/55–61°F). The heat source may be a light bulb, heated plates or coils. Not essential, but a useful piece of equipment to have and they are usually inexpensive to run.

Deciding what to grow

Gardeners want to grow their own vegetables for a variety of reasons. You may, for example, wish to control what you eat, which means growing produce organically and avoiding the use of potentially harmful chemicals and fertilizers necessary for higher yields of commercial production. There is also the pleasure of eating garden-fresh produce.

Home-grown vegetables have a fullness of flavour that is lost in shop-bought food. Another attractive aspect to growing them is the opportunity to experiment by producing more exotic and unusual fruit and vegetables that are either not available in most shops or are just too expensive to buy.

The ornamental potager

There is no reason why your vegetable garden should be any less attractive than the flower garden. A mixture of vegetables and herbs laid out in a square design, with perhaps an edging of clipped boxwood, will turn the edible garden into an object of beauty. You can make a very simple square design with just a few rows of vegetables or opt for a series of squares, with brick paths in between each square, to make a more elaborate potager. Herbs are ideally suited to this kind of design, and your potager could devote one or two squares to them. Site such a potager near the house, to make access easier. Additionally, soft fruit, such as gooseberries, can be trained as ornamental standards, and tree fruit can be fan-trained on wire supports, taking up minimal space and adding to the attraction of the garden.

Growing your own
Vegetables and herbs not only taste good but can also look good if they are well laid-out.

Planning an attractive vegetable plot
Growing edible crops can be as satisfying visually as it is in culinary terms, as this elegant
vegetable plot demonstrates.

A year in the vegetable plot

EARLY SPRING

GENERAL TASKS

- Prepare seedbeds and cover with cloches or black polythene to warm up.
- Check beds are ready for the new season's crops and all weeds and roots have been removed.
- Feed over-wintered crops with a general fertilizer or mulch.
- Keep an eye on weeds and watch out for early signs of pests. Cover vulnerable plants with netting or fleece.
- Order seeds and young plants from mail-order companies.
- Check stored vegetables regularly and get rid of any that show signs of deterioration.
- This is the start of the busy season for sowing seeds, pricking out and potting on – check there is plenty of space in cold frames as well as the greenhouse and shed.

TIME TO SOW

In situ: American land cress, beetroot, broad beans, carrots, chicory (heading), kohl rabi, peas (earlies), radishes, rocket, spinach, spring onions, turnips.

In a nursery bed: Brussels sprouts (earlies), cabbage (autumn and winter), globe artichokes, leeks, lettuce.

Under glass: Aubergines, broccoli (calabrese), cauliflowers (summer), chard, celery, okra, onions, peppers, pumpkins, shallots, squashes, indoor tomatoes.

TIME TO PLANT/TRANSPLANT

In situ: Asparagus, cabbage (summer), cauliflower (summer), garlic, globe artichokes, Jerusalem artichokes, onions, potatoes (earlies), shallots.

Under glass: Early salad leaves, tomatoes.

IN SEASON

American land cress, Brussels sprouts, broccoli (sprouting), cabbages, cauliflowers, celeriac, celery (trench), chard, chicory (forced), lamb's lettuce, leeks, lettuces, parsnips, pumpkins, radishes, rhubarb (forced), spinach, spring onions, swedes, turnip tops.

LATE SPRING

GENERAL TASKS

- Begin to move young plants outside to start the hardening-off process.
- Keep an eye on the soil and water if it becomes very dry. Mulch when the soil is moist to help retain water.
- Hoe regularly to keep on top of weeds and check for signs of pests and disease – especially under cloches or fleece.
- Stay on top of thinning out, earthing up potatoes and providing support for climbers such as peas and beans.
- Clear beds of overwintered vegetables. Store remaining crops and add stumps, roots and any that are not good enough to keep to the compost heap.
- Prepare beds for new crops: put in supports for netting or wire cages; erect cane supports as required; dig a trench for celery and prepare planting holes for cucurbits.

TIME TO SOW

In situ: American land cress, asparagus, beetroot, broad beans, broccoli (calabrese), carrots, chard, chicory (heading and forcing), endive, fennel, kale, kohl rabi, lettuce, onions (bulbing and spring), parsnips, peas, spinach, radishes, rocket, swedes, turnips.

In a nursery bed: Brussels sprouts, cabbages (autumn and winter), cauliflowers (autumn and winter), kale, leeks, broccoli (sprouting).

Under glass: Beans (borlotti, French and runner), cardoon, courgettes, cucumbers, pumpkins, squashes, sweetcorn, tomatoes (outdoor).

TIME TO PLANT/TRANSPLANT
In situ: Asparagus, cabbage (summer), globe artichokes, Jerusalem artichokes, early brassicas, onions, potatoes.

Once all danger of frosts has passed: Aubergines, celeriac, celery, beans (borlotti, French and runner), peas (earlies), peppers, sweetcorn, tomatoes (outdoor).

Under glass: Aubergines, cucumbers, tomatoes.

IN SEASON
American land cress, asparagus, broad beans, broccoli (sprouting), Brussels sprouts, cabbages, carrots, cauliflowers, chard, kale, leeks, lettuce, radishes, rhubarb, salad onions, spinach, turnips, turnip tops.

EARLY SUMMER

GENERAL TASKS
- Sow intercrops such as lettuces where there is space. Lightly fork over the ground and add fertilizer first.
- Apply a general fertilizer or high-potash feed to plants that need it, such as squashes, cucumbers and tomatoes.
- Watch for pests and take precautions. Keep on top of watering and weeding.
- Stake, tie in and train sideshoots on crops like beans, cucumbers and tomatoes.
- Order in any seedlings or young plants needed for autumn and winter sowings.
- Start harvesting crops as they are ready.
- It's easy to forget at this time of year to continue with successive sowing to provide a continuous supply of

crops. Sow seeds in situ, or under cover for transplanting later.

TIME TO SOW
In situ: American land cress, beetroot, cardoon, carrots, chard, chicory (forcing and heading), courgettes, endive (frisée), fennel, kale, kohl rabi, lettuces, peas, radishes, salad onions, spinach, squashes, swedes, sweetcorn, turnips.

In a nursery bed: Winter brassicas.

TIME TO PLANT/TRANSPLANT
In situ: Beans (borlotti, French and runner), brassicas (autumn and winter), celery, cucumbers, globe artichokes, leeks, lettuces, okra, peppers, pumpkins, squashes, sweetcorn, tomatoes.

IN SEASON
Asparagus, broad beans, broccoli (calabrese), cabbages, carrots, cauliflowers, chard, lamb's lettuce, endive, kohl rabi, American land cress, lettuce, onions (salad and overwintered bulbs), peas, potatoes, radishes, rhubarb, spinach, turnips.

LATE SUMMER

GENERAL TASKS
- Keep picking repeat-producing crops such as beans, courgettes and tomatoes to encourage more to grow.
- Clear away crops that have finished and dig over the ground to expose any pests or weeds in the soil.
- Pests and diseases spread quickly in hot, dry weather, so stay vigilant. If it's wet and humid, watch for potato blight, which thrives in those conditions.
- If you have suitable space, plant up a green manure crop.
- Clear cold frames and the greenhouse ready for sowing and growing winter crops that need protection from frosts.
- Weed, mulch and water.

TIME TO SOW

In situ: American land cress, beetroot, carrots, chard, chicory (heading), Chinese cabbage, lamb's lettuce, endive (broad-leaved), fennel, kohl rabi, lettuce, mizuna greens, onions (bulbing and salad), pak choi, peas (autumn), radishes (summer and winter), spinach (winter), turnips.

In a nursery bed: Cabbage (spring and red varieties), kale.

TIME TO PLANT/TRANSPLANT

In situ: Broccoli (sprouting), cabbages (spring), cauliflowers (autumn and winter), kale, leeks.

IN SEASON

American land cress, aubergines, beetroot, borlotti beans, broad beans, broccoli (calabrese), cabbage, carrots, cauliflowers, celery, chard, lamb's lettuce, cucumbers, endive, French beans, garlic, globe artichokes, kohl rabi, leeks, lettuce, onions (bulbing), potatoes, radishes, runner beans, salad onions, shallots, spinach, squashes, sweetcorn, tomatoes, turnips.

EARLY AUTUMN

GENERAL TASKS

- Cover late and overwintering crops with cloches or fleeces if the weather turns cold.
- Clear spent crops and supports from beds ready for autumn digging and liming.
- Cover root vegetables that are being left in the ground with straw, or lift and store in a frost-free place.
- Start gathering together used pots, seed trays, labels, canes, etc. and clean and store ready for future use.

TIME TO SOW

In situ: Broad beans, carrots, peas, rocket, spinach (winter).

In a nursery bed: Cabbages (spring), cauliflowers (summer).

Under glass: Lettuces, mizuna greens, pak choi, radishes.

TIME TO PLANT/TRANSPLANT

In situ: Cabbages (spring), garlic, onions (autumn).

Under glass: Lettuces.

IN SEASON

Aubergines, beetroot, broccoli (calabrese and sprouting), Brussels sprouts, cabbages, cardoons, carrots, cauliflowers, celeriac, celery, chicory (heading), cucumbers, endive, fennel, French beans, Jerusalem artichokes, kale, kohl rabi, leeks, lettuces, mizuna greens, okra, onions, pak choi, parsnips, peas, peppers, potatoes, pumpkins, radishes, runner beans, spinach, squashes, swedes, sweetcorn, tomatoes, turnips.

LATE AUTUMN

GENERAL TASKS

- Clear all non-hardy crops and dig over the ground. If it's heavy leave clods on top to allow the frost to break it down.
- Lift and store any remaining winter crops that are at risk of severe weather. Check any stored crops are still in good condition.
- Earth up stems of cabbages, cauliflowers and Brussels sprouts to protect from wind rock.
- Gather leaves together to make your own nutritious leafmould to use as a mulch (it should be ready in a year). Erect a simple structure of wire netting wrapped around three or four stakes and pile in the leaves, pushing down firmly. Or pack them into black

plastic bags, punch in a few holes and leave to rot down – this may take longer than a year.

TIME TO SOW

In situ: Broad beans, carrots, peas.

Under glass: Lettuces, mizuna greens, pak choi, radishes, rocket.

TIME TO PLANT/TRANSPLANT

In situ: Cabbages (spring), garlic, onions (autumn).

IN SEASON

American land cress, Brussels sprouts, cabbages, carrots, cauliflowers, celeriac, celery, chard, chicory (heading and forced), Chinese cabbage, lamb's lettuce, endive, fennel, kohl rabi, Jerusalem artichokes, kale, leeks, lettuce, mizuna greens, okra, pak choi, parsnips, potatoes, pumpkins, radishes, rhubarb, spinach, swedes, turnips.

WINTER

GENERAL TASKS

- Carry on with digging and preparing soil as weather permits.
- Continue to check stored crops regularly for signs of mould, pests or diseases.
- Clean cloches and cold frames that are not in use.
- If bad weather is forecast, lift a supply of fresh vegetables so you do not need to do so in the snow or frost.
- Check compost bins: empty them out, mix the contents together, then refill.
- Put out cloches, cold frames, black polythene or straw to warm up beds ready for early plantings.
- Clean and sharpen tools for the start of the new gardening year. Check over equipment – including sundry items such as seed trays, canes, labels, string, etc. – replacing or supplementing where needed.
- On a fine day, walk round your plot to remind yourself of the year's successes and failures, making

notes if necessary, to help plan next year's crops and rotations. Order in seeds and young plants.

TIME TO SOW

Under glass: Aubergine, beetroot, broad beans, cabbages (summer), carrots, cauliflowers (summer), celeriac, celery, cucumbers, leeks, lettuces, onions, radishes, salad onions, spinach.

TIME TO PLANT/TRANSPLANT

In situ: Garlic, globe artichokes, rhubarb, shallots.

IN SEASON

American land cress, broccoli (sprouting), Brussels sprouts, cabbages, carrots, cauliflowers, celeriac, celery, chicory (forced and heading), lamb's lettuce, endive, fennel, Jerusalem artichokes, kale, kohl rabi, leeks, lettuces, mizuna greens, pak choi, parsnips, radishes, rhubarb (forced), spinach, swedes.

Choosing and buying plants

How long crops take to grow, whether continuity is required, how much time is available and the skill of the gardener are all major considerations when planning a vegetable garden, since these will influence the time needed to tend the plot. Inexperienced gardeners should try not to be too ambitious at first and thus risk disappointment; they should start with fast-maturing salad crops.

As gardeners become more experienced and skilled, they can gradually experiment with vegetables that are more difficult to grow. One advantage of short-term crops is that they often allow several cropping cycles in each year, which is a quick way to gain tangible results – and if something does go wrong, the mistakes will have no long-term implications.

Buying plants

Make a list of all the plants that you want to grow and stick to it. Remember that plants get bigger; don't worry if the beds look a bit bare when first planted, as they will soon fill out.

Fast-growing crops
Quick-maturing carrots and beetroots allow you to re-use the space within one growing year.

The most important thing to consider when growing any vegetable is the direction of the sun. In the northern hemisphere, if a garden or vegetable plot faces south, is sheltered, and the general climate is hot enough, heat-loving vegetables can be grown. If the vegetable plot faces north, then you should concentrate on those plants that will flourish in a degree of shade.

It is important to plan purchasing and planting carefully. Make a list of the vegetables that you plan to grow then check whether there is a specialist nursery near you. If there is you can purchase the plants you require in person, but you may have to order them to be sent by mail. Nurseries are well used to sending plants through the post and it is seldom that plants arrive in anything other than good condition.

It is best to buy plants and seeds from a specialist nursery rather than from a general garden centre or supermarket where the choice may be limited and, usually, no specialist advice or help is available.

Bare-root plants

Plants should be planted at the right time of the year and this applies particularly to vegetables. Generally these are always best planted in the autumn when the growth is dying down but there remains enough warmth and moisture in the soil to let the root system establish itself. Also, for fruit trees you are better to purchase bare-root plants than trees and shrubs that have been container-grown, as these will generally be healthier and in better condition overall.

Plants grown in open soil and lifted as 'bare root' plants often do much better than those raised and bought in plastic containers. Plants raised in containers often have restricted root systems which never fully recover even when planted out. Bare root plants are only available when they are dormant, in the winter time, so this does restrict when you can plant them.

Heeling in

If you cannot plant large vegetables as soon as they arrive, dig a small trench in a container, lay the plants in it at an angle of 45 degrees and cover them firmly with soil until you have time to complete the planting properly. The vegetables are unlikely to come to too much harm if they are not left for too long. If a frost threatens, protect the plants by covering them with garden fleece or some sacking.

Buying plants in person

If you plan to buy young vegetable plants yourself at a garden centre, rather than growing them from seed, there are a number of things to look out for. Check all the leaves for signs of pests or disease (see pages 44–5), and make sure that the plant does not suffer from leaf drop. Avoid plants that have moss growing on the top of the container, as this indicates that they have been there for too long. Check to see that there are not too many roots growing out of the holes at the foot of the container for the same reason.

Plug plants (young vegetable plants, usually sold in packs of six) are a great, easy way to grow vegetables and especially helpful if you're just starting out or haven't much time. The choice will be more limited but the more tricky jobs of sowing seeds and pricking out are done for you.

Slow-growing crops
Slower-maturing maincrop potatoes and onions occupy a section of the plot for most of the year.

Designing your plot

Many people grow vegetables only if they can find some spare room in the garden, while for others the challenge is to produce a year-round supply of home-grown food. The planning and layout of a vegetable plot and types of vegetable chosen will be influenced by the number of people who want to eat home-grown vegetables, and the vegetables they like the most.

It should be possible to keep a family of three supplied with vegetables year-round from a plot measuring around 7x4m (21x12ft), but a good supply of produce can actually be grown on an area much smaller than this. Where space is limited, greater yields can be produced by plants that grow vertically rather than those that spread sideways.

Choosing a suitable site

The ideal site in which to grow vegetables is one that is warm and sunny during the growing season, and has plenty of light and good air circulation, while being sheltered from strong winds (since wind exposure can reduce plant growth by up to 30 per cent). The air flow is particularly important for wind-pollinated crops, such as sweet corn, and to reduce the incidence of pests and diseases, which is worse in still air conditions. A gently sloping, sunny site is perfect for an early start in spring, because it will warm up slightly quicker than other aspects. On steeper slopes, plant across the slope rather than down it, because this will reduce soil erosion during heavy rain.

Planning the vegetable plot

An efficient vegetable garden should be planned to make the best use of sun, shelter and space. The vegetables should be planted in rotation groups (see pages 28–9) to ensure pests do not build up.

It is important that you organize your vegetable plot as efficiently as possible, to ensure that the crops are rotated correctly and that you make the maximum use of the available sun and shelter.

Plant the tallest crops (such as Jerusalem artichokes or scarlet runners) so that they do not block the light from the smaller-growing vegetables. Use the walls or fences for shelter, and for supports for beans, peas or cordon or espalier fruit trees.

Remember to leave yourself ample space to walk between the blocks or rows of vegetables. Trampling on the soil will destroy its structure, and reduce its potential yield.

Growing in containers

Vegetables, fruit and herbs can all be grown in containers in the most unlikely of places – on patios, balconies, fire escapes and walkways, or on any small plot of ground where the light is good. You can even grow some vegetables on your windowsill!

Although you will naturally want to choose the most attractive container for your vegetables, for successful results the container's appearance is not nearly as important as the contents. Whatever the plant to go in the container, you need to fill it with fresh, well-balanced potting mix and a base dressing of fertilizer, adding further top-dressings of fertilizer throughout the growing season. Long-rooted vegetables such as carrots and parsnips require deep containers (at least 45cm/18in deep) in order to grow satisfactorily.

Tall crops tend to become unstable, especially if grown in small pots, and can blow over in strong winds, so protect these with stones or netting. Container-grown crops need to be watered frequently during warm or dry weather.

Organic gardening

You can help to achieve harmony in your garden by working with nature to replenish its resources as you make use of them. You can do this by feeding the soil with plant waste such as decaying grass cuttings or autumn leaves that provide beneficial micro-organisms. This is what organic gardening is all about – growing vegetables, herbs, flowers or ornamental plants using plant matter, compost and beneficial insects rather than synthetic products such as pesticides and fertilizers.

Compost bins are an essential part of organic vegetable gardening. Raw kitchen scraps as well as leaves and cuttings from the garden can all go into the bins.

Growing vegetables from seed

Seed is the means by which most vegetables reproduce themselves. Among all the methods of propagation that can be used with vegetables, growing from seed is the most common. It is much less expensive than buying already established plants, although the disadvantage is the amount of time involved in preparing and planting the seeds and then waiting for them to grow.

Many different kinds of vegetable are normally grown from seed. Vegetable seeds can vary enormously in size and can either be sown directly into the ground or sown in pots or seed trays and transplanted later. Seed packets will advise you on which method is most suitable for the vegetable of your choice. It can depend on how you will use the vegetable and the quantity you would like. Growing from seed is generally straightforward, but it is important to understand a little of their requirements.

DIRECT SOWING

Many vegetables can be sown directly into the ground where they are to grow. However, to achieve success and to have as many seeds germinate as possible, you must first ensure that the timing and conditions are just right. So the temperature must be suitable – most vegetables simply will not grow

1 Prepare a seedbed by clearing any existing weeds, making a reasonably fine bed without too many soil lumps or stones.

2 Mark out different areas for the vegetables to be planted using sand. Vegetables don't have to be grown in rows; a prettier arrangement might be more suitable for a garden setting.

Seed requirements

Seeds have certain basic requirements in order to germinate and grow.

- Moisture is supplied by moist compost or soil. Larger seeds can be soaked overnight to speed up their germination time.
- Oxygen is available in a well-aerated seed or potting compost, or in soil that is well cultivated. Waterlogged or compacted soil can cause failure.
- Warmth is required in varying degrees for successful germination. The optimum temperature is 20°C (68°F).
- Some seeds, particularly those of wild plants, require light to germinate. As a general rule, most small seeds should be surface sown or only lightly covered. Bury larger seeds to their own depth.

Germination time

On average, germination takes up to 30 days, but some seeds may take 90 days or more. If your seeds do not come up in reasonable time, take a look at them to find out what has gone wrong. In some cases the seed may have rotted or gone soggy, in which case start again. If the seed is hard, it is still alive and is in dormancy, awaiting the right conditions to germinate. Seeds do this in order to give themselves the best chance of survival; without such safety mechanisms they might germinate during drought or when temperatures are too high or too low for survival. To improve their chance of survival, wild seeds do not always germinate all at the same time. This may give rise to erratic germination over a long period.

unless the average temperature during the day is above 6°C (43°F) – the soil must be well prepared and you must follow the seed company's guidelines

as to planting depth and distance. In order for the seeds to germinate the earth must be warm enough and neither too dry nor too wet.

 Sprinkle seeds over the soil. Dustlike seeds should be scattered on the surface. Larger seeds should be pressed into the soil, to the same depth as the seed size. Sow sparsely to avoid having to thin out the seedlings.

4 If the seeds need to be covered (see step 3), use your fingers or a small fork to work them lightly into the soil. Firm the soil down lightly and water with a fine rose.

Cold treatment or stratification

Some seeds will not germinate until they have been through the low and freezing temperatures of winter. In this way, nature ensures that they germinate in spring, when weather conditions are most favourable for growth. Sow these seeds in the autumn, cover the tray with glass to protect against mice and birds, and leave it outside or in a cold frame over the winter. Germination will take place in early or late spring.

Alternatively, mix the seed with moist peat or sand in a plastic bag and leave outside over the winter (or in the refrigerator for approximately eight weeks). In the spring, sow as normal.

The seeds of some vegetables are contained in a fleshy coating. To germinate, the seed coat has to be broken down. In nature this happens when the seed passes through a bird's intestine. If you want to grow such seeds yourself, they should be stratified over winter, although some may take as long as two seasons to germinate.

Scarification

Seeds with very hard coats take a long time to germinate unless you break down the seed coat so the seed can absorb moisture. This treatment is called scarification. The easiest method is to soak the seeds in warm water for 24 hours.

Where the seed coat is very hard, you may have to wear it down in one of two ways:
Scraping Place small seeds in a jar lined with sandpaper and shake the jar.
Chipping Using a sharp knife, make a nick in the outer coat of large seeds.

Do not damage the inner, soft material, the part of the seed that will germinate, or the seed may rot.

INDOOR SOWING

Because some vegetables have tiny seeds and germination can take many weeks, even months in some cases, it is not always practical to sow in situ. Vermin or birds may take the seed; more usually, weed growth overtakes the sowing area, and distinguishing between weed and vegetable seedlings

1 Prepare the seed tray with special seed and sowing compost, level it off 0.6 cm (¼in) below the rim. Water with a fine rose until moist throughout.

2 Pour the seeds into the palm of your hand, pick some up between your thumb and forefinger, and sprinkle thinly and evenly over the surface of the seed tray. Do not sow too thickly.

Caring for seedlings

After direct sowing, always mark the area with sticks or stones or by sprinkling clean sand over the seeded area and label with the date and plant name.

If the season is windy, hot, or cold, you should cover the area with 'fleece' to protect the seeds and prevent the soil from drying out. A featherlight, translucent fibre covering fleece creates a warm microclimate and allows rain through; it also keeps off birds and pests.

Seed sown indoors

Seed trays should be kept in the shade, never in direct sun. Keep them in a warm place in the house or in a greenhouse.

When the seeds start to germinate, remove the glass cover. Do not overwater the seedlings or allow the seed compost to dry out. Keep them out of direct sun; high temperatures encourage spindly growth.

Because the seedlings have been growing in a protected environment, they need to be gradually acclimatized to conditions out of doors. This process is known as 'hardening off'. For a period of two to three weeks move the seedlings from the greenhouse to a closed frame or open the frame during the day, putting them back in the protected environment at night.

Transplant the seedlings into small pots when they are large enough to handle. Allow them to become well rooted before planting.

Self-seeding

Some vegetables will self-seed if the flower heads are left for the seed to mature. In any natural or ecological planting this is desirable. Unwanted seedlings can be transplanted or hoed out.

can be difficult. It is often best to germinate small seeds in controlled conditions indoors, in a seed tray rather than in the open ground.

3 Lightly cover with fine seed compost sieved through a plastic pot or sieve. Cover larger seeds to their own thickness or press them into the seed compost. Tiny seeds germinate best uncovered. Water gently with a fine rose.

4 Cover the seed tray with a sheet of glass or a plastic lid. This keeps moisture in, helps to eliminate the need for further watering, and prevents pests attacking the seeds and emerging seedlings. Keep in the shade.

Preparing the site

Just as ploughing is the farmer's way of moving the soil deeply in preparation for shallower cultivations and seed-sowing, digging is the basic cultivation of the gardener. You must dig any ground that is being cultivated for the first time or that has just been cleared of an old crop. A spade is the normal tool used for digging, but on heavy ground, a strong fork is much easier to use and just as effective.

The ideal soil for growing vegetables is a loam (a mixture of clay, sand, and silt in more or less equal proportions) containing humus (decaying organic matter) and with a pH, or acidity level, preferably between 6.5 and 7.0. Soils that vary from this ideal – that is, they are more sandy, or have little humus – may need more cultivation. Soil also needs to be fertile,

which usually means adding fertilizers or well-rotted manure before sowing or planting (see pages 38–9).

There are several reasons for digging. The main one is to break up the soil so that excess water can drain away and roots can penetrate in their search for water and nutrients. As the ground is broken up, air is able to reach down into it so that the roots can 'breathe'.

DIGGING THE SOIL

The depth of your topsoil, the quality of drainage in your garden and whether or not your plot has been previously cultivated, will all determine the

best digging method to use. Single and double digging are the most effective and labour-efficient digging techniques for areas of ground. For single

1 When single digging a plot of land, use a line to mark out the position of the first trench. The trench should be 23–25cm (9–10in) wide.

2 Dig out the soil to a full spade's depth and barrow it away to the far end of the plot, where it will be used to fill in the final trench.

Digging also creates a suitable tilth for sowing or planting and is the most thorough and reliable way of burying bulky organic matter, such as garden compost, that is vital if the soil is to 'live' and support good crops.

Basic cultivation

In order to grow worthwhile crops, you need at least a basic knowledge of soil cultivation and the tools required to carry it out. As well as a spade and fork, you will need a good, sturdy rake to break down the soil surface still further before sowing seeds. When sowing seeds or planting out seedlings, always use a garden line; never rely on drawing out a straight line by eye, as it will nearly always end up not being straight at all if you use this method.

Once the plants are growing, they will inevitably be challenged by weeds. The easiest way of dealing with these is to hoe them out, using either a Dutch or a draw hoe. Never try to cultivate the ground when it is wet enough to stick to the tools and always clean your tools after use. All garden tools can be made of either ordinary or stainless steel. Stainless steel costs more, but does not go rusty. As a general rule, always buy the best tools you can afford; the better they are, the longer they will last. If you maintain them properly as well, so much the better.

If the soil conditions are not suitable for the plants you want to grow, your results will be poor. Within the soil the most important material is the organic matter or humus. In nature this comes from decomposed vegetation, but in the garden you must add it in the form of garden compost or farmyard manure. Normal levels of organic matter contain only small amounts of the essential plant foods, so you will need to add these in the form of fertilizers. Under average garden conditions, add both bulky organic matter and plant foods to the soil at least once a year for it to remain in a suitable state for plants to grow well.

digging, follow the sequence shown here. Before commencing any digging, make sure that the site to be dug is clear of all persistent weeds, in order to reduce the competition that young plants face in their first weeks in the soil, when they need to bed in and establish themselves properly.

3 Turn around, so you have your back to the plot to be dug, and start on the next trench, turning this soil into the first trench.

4 Always keep the trench open and clear so that there is enough room to accommodate the next 'row' of soil excavated from the previous trench.

Fertilizing the soil

For optimum results, soil that is intensively cultivated needs generous fertilizing. This can be provided with organic or inorganic matter. A great advantage of organic manures and fertilizers is that they encourage worm activity, which in turn aids soil fertility. Soil that has had no organic matter added is likely to have a worm count of 100–300 per sq m (sq yd) in the top 30cm (12in) of soil. This figure often increases to around 400–500 per sq m (sq yd) if organic matter is regularly added.

Although quite adequate crops of vegetables can be grown in soils where only organic manure and fertilizers are used, higher yields are usually achieved where inorganic, 'chemical' fertilizers are incorporated. The amount of fertilizer needed will depend on the soil type, because light, sandy soils lose fertilizer quickly, whereas clay soils will hold nutrients for much longer. It is also affected by the kind of crop being grown: leafy crops, such as cabbages, need plenty of nitrogen, with one-third of this being provided when they are planted and the remaining two-thirds supplied while the plants are growing.

Vegetable crops growing through winter should get most of their nitrogen in spring rather than autumn, because nitrogen encourages soft growth, and if large quantities of nitrogen are added in autumn this could lead to the soft growth being killed by frost. Therefore, overwintering crops should be given a balanced fertilizer to toughen the leaves and stems. Fruiting crops such as tomatoes and peppers need regular fertilizing with phosphate and potassium fertilizers as soon as the plants start to flower in order to encourage good flower and fruit development.

Preparing the soil

The aim of tasks such as digging and raking the soil is to get the soil into the best condition possible for growing vegetables. Digging is the most important of these operations, because it allows air into the soil. This encourages the biological activity so essential for soil fertility, as well as raising clods of earth so that they can be broken up by frost.

IMPROVING SOIL

While we cannot completely change the basic soil type we have in the garden and must learn to live with it to a degree, we can temporarily alter its pH (by adding lime), feed it and improve its structure. The aim is to end up with soil rich in humus with a top layer of fine, crumbly tilth. Even if your soil is

1 Organic compost made from organic garden waste is an invaluable source of nutrients. Check that the compost is well rotted before you put it on the ground, as fresh compost will burn any plants it comes into contact with.

2 Spread a thick layer of well-rotted organic matter onto the soil surface. Use a spade or fork to remove the compost from the wheelbarrow and then rake it evenly all over the area to be cultivated.

No-dig method

Growing methods involving little or no cultivation are very popular, especially on light soils where the soil structure is easily damaged or where natural fertility is low. The no-dig, or 'zero-cultivation', technique uses the resident worm population to cultivate the soil; layers of well-rotted organic matter are spread over the soil as a mulch and the worms incorporate this into the soil. Thus no digging is needed. Crop plants are inserted through the mulch, and when they have matured, the stalks are cut off at soil level and the new crop is planted between the rows of the previous crops, while the roots rot in situ.

Deep-dig method

The deep-digging method of soil preparation involves incorporating large amounts of compost or manure while double-digging a plot. This creates a deep, fertile rooting zone for the plants. Further dressings of organic matter are added at regular intervals, but there is no need for additional digging.

Difficult soils

The no-dig and deep-dig methods are ideal if you have a heavy soil that suffers from compaction when cultivated in wet conditions (although this problem may be overcome by working on wooden boards laid on the soil) or a light, sandy soil needing humus and fertility. These soils benefit from the lack of cultivation and the large amount of organic matter that is added.

Crops such as onions and lettuce, which can be planted close together, will usually do particularly well when they are cultivated in these kinds of soil.

Preparing a seedbed

Digging alone would leave the soil too uneven for growing most vegetables, so further cultivation is needed to produce a fine crumb structure, or 'tilth', on the soil surface. This usually involves raking the soil several times to break down any lumps, and removing any stones you find, to create a fairly level, even surface.

naturally neutral and fertile, it will need a certain amount of organic material in order to remain so. While plants may grow happily in this type of soil in

the first year, they will suck the nutrients out of it. The soil must be constantly replenished if you want to carry on getting a good harvest.

3 Dig the bed thoroughly with a garden fork, incorporating the compost and working it into the soil beneath the surface. The final bed should have a slightly domed surface, ready to receive the plants.

4 The bed is now ready for planting. Carefully remove the plants from their pots. Use a hand trowel to dig a hole to the depth of the rootball and place the plant in it. Backfill the hole and gently firm soil around the base of the plant.

Planting techniques

Vegetables tend to be relatively short-term crops, because most grow rapidly and are harvested before they reach maturity. There are various ways in which you can maximize the efficiency of your vegetable plot in order to achieve the best possible yield of a number of different crops at all times.

Planning to avoid a glut

Take care when planning your garden not to grow too many of one type of vegetable that will ripen all at the same time. Do not overestimate your requirements.

Try to time your planting to produce a staggered harvest. For example, in the summer you may only wish to eat a lettuce every other day – that is, seven in a fortnight; don't therefore plant a dozen F1 hybrids that will mature at the same time, instead plant six and another six a fortnight later.

Some crops, particularly the short-term salad crops, are the most susceptible to gluts and gaps, but this can be avoided to a large extent by sowing batches of seed on a planned basis. Timing of sowings can be difficult to gauge, but a good guide is to choose the date when you hope to harvest the crop and count back from there the number of weeks needed for the plants to grow. Most of the information for this simple exercise will be given on the back of the seed packet.

To make the maximum use of the available soil, some vegetables, such as cabbages, cauliflowers and leeks, can be grown in a seedbed until they are large enough to transplant, and then they can be planted in their cropping area. This is a very helpful technique that can be introduced on a wide range of vegetables, and is invaluable for plants that would otherwise occupy the ground for a long period of time at a wide plant spacing. The disadvantage of transplanting young plants is that the disruption may check their growth unless they are kept well watered so that they establish and grow quickly. This is particularly critical where the transplants are dug up from a seedbed and replanted; some roots will always be damaged by this process, and a good supply of water is essential to help these plants recover. If they are short of water, many vegetables will 'bolt' – that is, the plant will stop growing leaves and develop instead a flower-bearing stem in an attempt to produce seeds.

A timing guide to successional sowings is to make the next sowing when the previous sowing has germinated and emerged through the soil.

Crop rotation

When groups of related vegetables are grown on a different plot from year to year, this is called crop rotation. One reason for moving crops from one part of the plot to another is to avoid the build-up of diseases and pests in the soil. Another benefit is that the soil's fertility can be improved by growing crops that add nitrogen, such as peas and most beans. Start by making a list of the various vegetables you intend to grow, and then classify them into groups based on their needs in terms of space and growth patterns.

Allocate each rotation group to a plot of land, and draw up a month-by-month cropping timetable. This will keep the land fully occupied and provide continuity. For example, after Brussels sprouts and leeks are finished in early spring, follow with sowings of peas, carrots, lettuces or bunching onions.

If you prefer, the vegetables can be from different crop groupings, which means that the rotation from one plot to another is a gradual process, rather than a wholesale changeover on a certain date.

If there is not enough space in a small garden to rotate entire blocks of vegetable crops, you could grow the plants in narrow strips instead and then regularly swop the groups between the strips.

Grouping the different types of vegetables together makes crop management easier. Leave at least two years before planting any vegetable from the same group on the same ground.

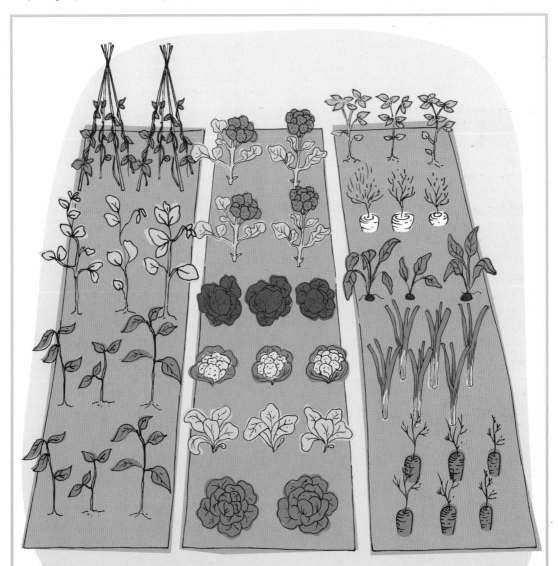

Crop rotation groups
This plot is divided into three groups: peas and beans (left), brassicas and leafy crops (middle), and roots and stems (right). A fourth, permanent, plot can be created for crops that are not shifted, such as asparagus. Each group is moved each year onto a new strip of land.

Multirow bed system

Where space is limited, a special, multirow bed system can be introduced. This has more, narrower beds than a conventional plot, and several rows of plants are grown more closely together than usual. With this multirow system, the beds are only 0.9–1.5m (3–5ft) wide and the centre of the bed can be reached from a path, so there is no need to walk on the soil and possibly crush it when tending plants. For several rows the plants are grown close together, with the distance between the rows being the same as the distance between the plants.

With such close spacing more plants can be grown per square metre (square yard) than by using a conventional system, in which plants are usually grown 45–60cm (1–2ft) apart. In the multirow system the pathways, at 60–75cm (2–2½ft) across, are slightly wider than those on the conventional system, which are generally about 45cm (1½ft) across.

By growing plants closer together, the competition for space between plants can be used to restrict the ultimate size of the individual vegetables. This can mean that having a small vegetable plot works as an advantage, and often the close spacing of plants reduces the amount of weeding necessary because the weeds are smothered.

However, such close planting does not work with all vegetables: lettuces, for example, will not form good hearts if they are grown at close spacings, unless a naturally small cultivar is chosen.

Making the best use of available space
Summer and winter cabbages are interspersed in rows. As one row is harvested before the other, there is room for the remainder to grow on.

Intercropping

The space between crops that are slow growing or need a wide spacing can be used to grow quick-maturing crops such as radishes, lettuces, kohl rabi or turnips, which are harvested before the main crop is large enough to fill its allotted space.

However, careful timing is important.

Such gaps between crops within a bed can also prove invaluable as seedbeds for other vegetables, which will later need to be transplanted into permanent positions at much wider spacings.

Maximum yields
Radishes and turnips make excellent catch crops when planted at the same time as later-maturing brassicas.

Extending the season

By making the most of your plot you can harvest crops year-round. This can be achieved by careful planning and successional sowings, growing several types of the same crop and protecting the plants from frost. If protection is used carefully and effectively, the growing season can be advanced throughout spring or run well into the autumn and winter months.

For raising young plants, a cold frame with a glass or plastic top can be used to acclimatize them before they are planted out. Plastic sheeting and polytunnels warm the soil before planting and are invaluable for protecting young or overwintering plants. Floating mulches, such as fleece, laid over the crop or suspended on hoops, will also protect early crops.

Growing under glass

To establish early crops, a large number of vegetables, such as leeks and brassicas, can be sown in containers in a greenhouse. Other crops, like cucumbers and melons, need such a frost-free environment at all times.

Plants dislike very hot temperatures, so apply a shading paint to the glass in late spring and always ensure that the greenhouse is well ventilated during the day. Plants will require copious watering.

Using growbags

Growbags contain a peat-based compost with added nutrients sufficient to establish most plants. Plants grown in growbags will need additional feeding throughout the year.

Traditionally growbags were used to grow outdoor tomatoes and placed against a warm wall with canes to which the plants could be trained. However, the range of vegetables that can be cultivated in growbags is actually much larger. Suitable vegetables include lettuces, peas, French beans, spinach or perpetual beetroot. Peas can be allowed to sprawl over the sides of the bag rather than being trained upwards on twigs. This also serves to hide the bags.

Forcing crops
Tuck in plastic sheeting with an edging iron over soil that needs warming before planting.

Hardening off young plants
Gradually open the cold frame lid to harden off young plants.

Gardening with growbags is simplicity itself. Put the bag in position and make a number of holes in the base according to the instructions on the side. Cut out the squares on the top of the bag and insert the plants. A normal bag can cultivate three tomato plants, but if you plan to use one for lettuces or peas then these can be planted quite densely. Plants need to be fed regularly with liquid fertilizer. Aim to cover the whole surface of the growbag when the plants are mature.

Growbag problems

There are two main problems with growbags. They need to be watered properly every day in summer:

modern bags often incorporate a plastic funnel that conveys water along the length. They need also to be concealed for they are not things of any great beauty.

If you have an established patio kitchen garden then you can construct special boxes or troughs into which new bags can be placed each year or you can have a sunken space on the terrace the right dimensions to take a new bag. This is an excellent idea if you are planning to grow vegetables, such as peas or tomatoes in growbags each year, for it lowers the bag to ground level making it less conspicuous and trailing plants will hide the plastic relatively quickly.

Watering growbags
Tomatoes are perfect for growing next to a sunny wall in a growbag. They will need watering often, especially in hot weather.

Growing under cover

Growing vegetables under cover, whether under glass or plastic, allows gardeners to extend both their repertoire of vegetables and the length of the season in which they can be grown. Yields are generally higher under cover and the quality better. Wind and storms need not be a worry and pests, such as rabbits, birds, cabbage root fly and carrot fly, can be easily excluded, while others such as whitefly and red spider mite can be more effectively controlled.

The ideal form of winter protection for vegetables is a greenhouse. However, many gardeners do not have room for such a large item. Fortunately, where space is a problem, low mini polytunnels, cold frames, lantern lights and cloches can perform part of a greenhouse's functions. Albeit on a much smaller scale, they will still be able to heat up the soil and offer light and warmth, plus protection from extremes of weather and many pests.

Polytunnels

Plastic polytunnels provide many of the advantages of a greenhouse and are a fraction of the price. They can be erected in a couple of hours and then taken down and stored when not required – although they can be a bit of an eyesore.

However, if you have the space in your garden then polytunnels will enable you to produce crops a good six weeks ahead of those grown in the open, which means you will be able to raise two crops a year instead of one. Low polytunnels are particularly useful as protection for crops prone to flying pests, birds and carrot flies. These can be homemade with a length of tough polythene, galvanized wire hoops and some twine and posts.

In very cold weather, protect overwintering plants – such as broad beans – with a plastic tunnel.

Cold frames

The basic construction of a cold frame consists of a box with wooden or brick sides, covered over with a glass or plastic lid, often sloping. You can make a cold frame yourself quite easily by simply placing a sheet of plastic over a wooden box.

Cold frames are useful for hardening off greenhouse-grown plants and raising seedlings. They can also be used for growing tender plants, such as aubergines, peppers, melons and cucumbers, as well as protecting hardier crops.

To work to their full capacity, they should be put in a sheltered place where they get maximum exposure to the sun. On hot days, prop the lid open to prevent overheating, while during cold, frosty spells spread old carpet, sacking or newspaper over the top as insulation.

Cloches and lights

Cloches and lantern lights are simple plastic or glass tents, which are smaller than cold frames and portable, and as such are used to protect plants that are grown out. A glass cloche will hold the heat better than plastic, and being heavier it is less prone to being blown away. Glass is also less likely to become brittle and crack, although it is generally more delicate to handle.

Cloches and lights are useful for drying out and warming soil prior to planting, and will protect seedlings and hasten their growth. They will also harden off greenhouse-grown plants and, for older plants, they offer protection against pests, will speed up the ripening process and extend the growing season. They can even be used to protect some crops throughout winter.

Other forms of protection

Horticultural fleece and even a humble sheet of plastic film will also help out the vegetable gardener by warming and drying out soil, thereby protecting plants from extremes of cold and also pests. Horticultural fleece operates differently from plastic, as it allows light, air and water to pass through it, enabling plants to breathe. It is also lighter than plastic. Given all these characteristics it can be left on top of the crops as they mature, keeping off many pests and preventing wind damage.

An outside cover for onions. If they are pulled in wet weather let them dry before storing over the winter.

In very hard weather, containers can be wrapped in bubble wrap, weighed down with a stone.

Watering

Plants, whether they have just germinated or are heavily mature, must have water for growth. Most plants have critical periods when water is especially vital, so the skill in providing an optimum water supply is to know when and how to apply the water.

The amount of water your plants require depends upon weather and soil conditions, as well as the health of the individual plant. Young plants and seedlings need frequent light watering. Try to ensure that they get a good soak every few days – once plants are mature, frequent light watering simply encourages their roots to stay near the surface rather than growing deep down into the ground.

Leafy salad crops will need extra water in dry periods to prevent them from running to seed, while the fruiting vegetables need more attention in terms of watering when their flowers appear and when the fruits and pods are growing.

Follow these basic rules:
- At the seed and seedling stage, to aid establishment. Water the seed drills with a fine watering can until they have developed a deep root system.
- After transplanting, to aid re-establishment. Leave a slight depression in the soil at the base of each stem, then fill it with water.
- To produce crops. Fruiting crops such as tomatoes and runner beans most need water while flowering and when the fruit starts to swell. Leafy crops need heavy watering about 15 days before harvesting. Root crops should have a steady supply of water from sowing through to cropping.

A gravel container filled with water enables the plant to draw up the moisture it needs in a gradual way without the compost becoming waterlogged. This is the watering principle adopted in many greenhouses.

If a plant appears totally dead and dried out it is worth plunging the pot and plant in a bucket of water and leaving it there until the bubbles have stopped rising to the surface. There is a chance that it may well recover.

The best times to water vegetables are early mornings or evenings when the sun is less intense, reducing the amount of moisture lost to evaporation.

Watering container plants

Watering is the most important part of vegetable container gardening and without water the plants will die. If you can install an automatic watering system, this will solve all problems.

There is absolutely no point in attempting to grow plants in containers, outside, in the summer, unless you are able to water them every day. That is not to say that they have to be watered every day. If it rains all week you certainly won't, but if you go away on holiday for a fortnight and this coincides with a hot dry spell don't be surprised if half your vegetables are dead when you return.

Plants grown in containers need far more moisture than plants grown in the garden. A large container 90cm (36in) in diameter may lose up to 5 litres (1.1 gallons) of water each day through the leaves of the plants (transpiration) and evaporation from the container itself, when it is hot and sunny. Terracotta containers are more subject to evaporation than plastic ones, but you can overcome this if you line earthenware pots with plastic sheets when they are planted.

Watering systems

With a large vegetable garden it is well worth installing an automatic watering system. These are computer-controlled and if you have one then all worries about watering vanish. There are three main systems: overhead sprinklers, trickle tubes and capillary systems. All have their advantages and disadvantages. Overhead sprinklers are probably the cheapest to install but they use the most water. Trickle hoses are more expensive but more effective. They deliver water directly to the roots of the plants. Capillary systems are expensive but useful for large areas requiring frequent irrigation.

WATERING

Watering is essential especially in summer and needs to be done every day in hot dry weather. Fill the container to the brim and let the surplus water drain away. Do not just sprinkle the plant and container lightly with water. This will do more harm than good.

Be careful when you water any acid-loving plants growing in ericaceous compost if you live in a hardwater area, as the leaves can turn yellow if the acid level in the compost changes. Either add a small amount of flowers of sulphur to the water or collect rain water in a barrel outside and use that.

Feeding

Vegetables need additional feeding to produce good crops, particularly those that are grown in containers. Liquid fertilizer is the easiest type of feed to apply. Leafy, root and fruiting vegetables have different requirements.

Good soil preparation will go a long way towards ensuring your plants have enough nutrients. Plants growing in soil that has had a large amount of organic manure dug into it for several years should hopefully not need extra feeding. However, the process of building up soil fertility can take a while to establish and in the meantime you may find it necessary to apply organic or chemical fertilizers to aid crop growth.

Vegetables, more than ornamental plants, are greedy for nutrients from the soil; in their growing season they put on a great deal of growth and may need an extra boost of feed. Vegetables grown in containers are particularly susceptible to shortages because the area and soil volume in containers is limited and because they are watered more frequently so the soil may be leached. So container-grown vegetables need regular feeding to thrive and produce the best crops.

Check the feed necessary for each plant and take care to apply the correct fertilizer at each stage of the plant's growth. Growing plants need a nitrogen-based fertilizer but you should switch to a potash- (potassium) based fertilizer as the plants reach maturity.

Mix any liquid feeds carefully in a can or spray can that can be kept specially for the purpose. Always follow the maker's instructions on the packet or bottle and do not be tempted to increase the strength of the solution as this may do more harm than good.

Foliar feeds are most effective during the summer and should be applied to the leaves on the 'little and often' principle. Plants can be sprayed every fortnight with benefit. It is better to apply any foliar feeds with a small spray can as this is much more economical.

When to feed

If the soil is well nourished it should not need much additional fertilizer but a slow release feed in the spring is helpful to the young plants. During the growing season it might be necessary to use a quick-acting fertilizer as a boost. The quickest-acting feeds come in liquid form.

Liquid feeds

Liquid feeds are particularly useful for vegetables as they give a quick, easily accessible burst of nutrients during the growing season. These feeds are either designed to be applied to the soil or, for a very direct route into the plant, some are meant to be sprayed directly onto the leaves; these are called foliar feeds. With both of these it is very important to make sure that the mix is correct; if it is too strong it can burn leaves and young plants.

Check the instructions to see how often the plants need feeding and do not be tempted to over-feed the plants.

Slow and controlled release feeds

Slow release feeds are great for feeding the soil which will then feed the plants. These come in granular or powdered form and can be used in spring.

Controlled release feeds are granules that are mixed into the soil or compost. They are usually used in containers and some will keep providing feed for months on end and so provide a 'once a season' feed.

Basic chemistry

The three main nutrients required by plants are nitrogen (N), phosphorus (P) and potassium (K), and are often referred to by just those symbols, NPK. Nitrogen is essential for healthy leaf growth, phosphorus for the development of proper root systems and potassium promotes the production of flowers and fruit.

Plants also need a number of trace elements, the most important of which are manganese and magnesium. Nutrients are present in varying proportions in all fertilizers and foliar feeds and are marked on the label. A balanced fertilizer will contain them in equal proportions. Growmore, for instance, is a balanced 7:7:7 formula that is widely used. A high potash (potassium) feed is excellent for tomatoes and fruit when the plants are mature and bearing fruit, but all tender vegetables, such as peppers, require high nitrogen feeds when they are growing to help establish healthy plants.

General requirements

Nearly all vegetable crops need to be fed generously unless the soil they are growing in has been improved with organic manure over several years. They require nitrogen-based feeds when growth starts in spring followed by potassium-based fertilizer as the plants reach maturity. Apply fertilizers in liquid form during the growing season – use a liquid fertilizer or foliar feed. Slow-release granules, however, are invaluable. Add them to the soil at the start of the growing season and one application will serve many plants throughout the year.

Mulching

A weed is any plant growing in a place where it is not wanted. Many weeds cause problems just because they are so tough and versatile that they can adapt to a wide range of growing conditions. For this reason they must always be dealt with before they get out of control. The most effective way to prevent them from appearing in the first place is to use a mulch.

Mulching for weed control

Mulching is the practice of covering the soil around plants with a layer of material to block out the light and help trap moisture. In today's gardens, where plastics are commonplace, inorganic black plastic sheeting is often chosen. Though not inviting to look at, it can be hidden beneath a thin layer of more attractive natural, organic mulch.

As a general rule, organic mulches provide the bonus of improving the fertility of the soil, but inorganic mulches are more effective because they form a better weed barrier. To be fully effective as a barrier, organic mulches must be applied as a layer at least 10cm (4in) thick. Both organic and inorganic mulches tend to be less effective against established perennial weeds, unless an entire area can be sealed until the weeds have died out and planting is carried out through the mulch while it is in place. One way of clearing weedy ground in summer is to cover the soil with a mulch of clear or white plastic, sealed around the edges. Weeds are gradually killed by a combination of high temperatures and lack of carbon dioxide.

The plastic sheeting can be removed after a time and used elsewhere. The treated area is weed-free, ready to plant and cover with an organic mulch, such as shredded bark or gravel (see below).

Gravel mulch
Covering the soil with a mulch such as gravel will block out light and prevent weed seeds from germinating.

Weeding

Weeds compete directly with your vegetables for light, nutrients and water. They can also act as hosts to pests and diseases (see pages 44–5), which can spread as the season progresses. Groundsel, for instance, often harbours the fungal diseases rust and mildew, and sap-sucking aphids. Chickweed also plays host to aphids as well as red spider mites.

Perennial weeds

Digging up perennial weeds is an effective disposal system, provided that every bit of the root system is removed from the soil. If only a few weeds are present, try digging them out with a knife or trowel, but you must remove the top 5cm (2in) of root close to the surface, to prevent the weed from re-growing. This is a reliable means of eradicating weeds growing close to garden plants. In this situation, often no other weed control method would be effective without risking damage to plants growing nearby.

Clearing weeds

The simplest way to deal with weeds is to remove them physically, either by pulling or digging them out or, if they are small, hoeing them off at soil level.

The biggest problem with this method of control is that most weed seeds require exposure to light before they germinate. Often, when weeding disturbs the soil, more air is allowed into the surface layers and an ideal seedbed is created. Although the existing weed seedlings are destroyed, the weed growth cycle starts all over again. This problem is often worse when using rotovators, because they leave the surface layers of soil light and fluffy, making a perfect seedbed. Perennial weeds are increased, too, because they are chopped into pieces, each capable of re-growing.

The most effective way to clear weeds, especially established perennials, is to use a combination of cultural and chemical methods. Spray weeds in full growth with a chemical herbicide and, as they start to die, bury them when the area is dug over. When the new weed seedlings germinate, spray them with a chemical while they are most vulnerable.

Annual weeds

Clearing annual weeds with a hoe is quick and effective, but the timing is important. The hoeing must be done when the weeds are tiny and before they start producing seed.

Hoeing will sever the stems of young weeds from the root system just below soil level. This both prevents the stem from forming new roots and stops the roots from producing a new stem. When hoeing, make sure you always walk backwards to avoid treading weeds back into the soil.

There is an old saying, 'One year's seeds make seven years' weeds', which has now been endorsed by scientific research and proved to be remarkably accurate – unfortunately for gardeners.

Annual weeds are capable of producing a staggering total of 60,000 viable seeds per square yard, per year. The vast majority of these seeds are found in the uppermost 5cm (2in) of soil, but they will usually germinate only when exposed to sufficient light levels. This is why mulching (see opposite page), which covers the soil and blocks out light, has become such a widely popular method of weed control. The added benefit of mulching is that there is also little chance of contaminating the soil with chemical residue.

General care

It is important to ensure that your crops are not damaged by pests and diseases (see pages 44–5). To do this you can use organic or chemical methods.

Organic methods

Reaching for a chemical is not the only solution to an outbreak of pests or disease; there are many other preventative measures that can be taken. The first step is to grow healthy, vigorous plants because these seem less susceptible to attack, especially when there is also good garden hygiene (clean and healthy plants and materials) and crop rotation is carried out (see pages 28–9).

Physical barriers can be put in place to deny pests access to the crop: for example, lay mats around the bases of brassicas to keep cabbage root fly at bay, or cover your crops with fine nets, the edges of which should be buried in the soil to deter flying pests.

Traps of shallow dishes containing cola or beer can also be laid to entice crawling pests into them so they can be easily disposed of. Finally, organic sprays based on natural substances, such as rotenone, pyrethrum, insecticidal soaps and sulphur, are useful and very effective controls against a variety of pests and diseases.

Chemical methods

These can be very effective in pest and disease control, as long as they are used strictly according to the instructions on the container and are applied thoroughly. Their main drawbacks are:

• Some chemicals may kill beneficial insects as well as harmful ones.
• Certain chemicals are very long-lasting.
• Chemicals may taint the produce with residue.

Physical barriers
Nets will keep pests such as pheasants and pigeons off the crops. This is especially important when the plants are young.

Organic sprays
Lettuce plants are treated with a solution
of insecticidal soap to kill aphids.

Protective barriers
A layer of netting protects succulent young
vegetable plants from marauding birds.

Baited traps
Fill a sunken dish with beer to catch slugs and
snails. The sticks help any beetles to escape.

Wasp traps
Hanging from a plum tree, this jar full
of sweet-smelling liquid attracts wasps.

Pests and diseases

These are the major pests, diseases and other problems that affect vegetables. However, do not be alarmed, as although there are numerous things to be concerned about, your plants are unlikely to be troubled by all of these. For proven environmental reasons, there is a strong emphasis in these pages on non-chemical methods of control of the pests and diseases discussed.

Aphids

These are among the most troublesome of insect pests, particularly greenfly and blackfly, and they attack a wide range of plants. Wash off aphids with plain or soapy water, or spray with insecticidal soap if necessary.

Blight

Blight affects potatoes and outdoor tomatoes, especially in wet seasons. It can be identified by the brown patches which appear on the leaves and lead to rot. Prevent it by growing disease-resistant varieties, and control by spraying in the very early stages.

Blossom end rot

Blossom end rot affects tomatoes in particular, especially those grown in pots or growbags, as this problem is commonly caused by underwatering. The first sign is the appearance of black patches underneath the fruit, which then rot. It cannot be cured, only prevented by regular watering and feeding.

Caterpillars

The caterpillars of various moths and butterflies eat holes in the leaves of numerous vegetables. They are usually green, brown or grey and are generally hairy. Caterpillars are easily picked off and destroyed, or plants can be sprayed with an insecticide if necessary.

Clubroot

Cabbages, cauliflowers, sprouts, swedes and turnips are among the plants prone to this disease, which causes growths to appear on the roots, wilting and rot. Prevent by liming the soil and adhering to a strict rotation plan. As there is no cure, remove and burn all affected plants.

Cutworms

These caterpillars, the larvae of several different moths and greenish brown or greyish brown in colour, live in the soil and feed on roots and stem bases of plants, causing young plants to wilt and die. Remove any found during soil cultivations.

Damping off

This disease affects seedlings indoors, causing them to suddenly collapse and die. Damping off can spread rapidly and should be prevented by using sterilized compost and clean containers.

Earwigs

These night-feeding insects, easily recognized by their rear pincers, eat holes in vegetables' leaves, flowers and buds. Remove and destroy any pests. Spray plants with an insecticide if necessary.

Flea beetles

Flea beetles are tiny black insects which jump high into the air when disturbed, and will eat holes in the foliage of all types of brassicas. Prevent them becoming a problem by clearing away all plant debris, where they overwinter, and protecting with fleece. Early and late sowings are safe from attack. Dusting with derris powder is another solution.

Grey mould

This major fungal disease, also known as botrytis, can infect all top growth of plants – flowers, buds, leaves and stems – resulting in rotting. Cut off any affected parts of plants, back to healthy tissue.

Leaf spot

Many diseases show up as brown or black spots on the leaves of numerous vegetables. The spots vary in size and some are in the form of rings. The best control method is to pick off any leaves showing spots. Spray affected plants with a fungicide if necessary.

Mildew

The most common is powdery mildew, appearing as white powdery patches on the leaves of many plants. Remove affected leaves. Spray plants with a fungicide if necessary.

Red spider mite

There are several kinds of these microscopic spider-like creatures that feed by sucking the sap from the leaves of many plants, particularly under glass. This results in fine pale yellow mottling on the upper leaf surfaces. Spraying plants regularly with plain water will deter the mites. Or spray plants with insecticidal soap.

Root rot

Root rot primarily affects beans, peas, tomatoes, cucumbers and container-grown vegetables. It is a fungus which causes roots to turn black and the plants to wilt and die. Prevent the disease by practising crop rotation, using sterilized compost and watering with mains water. Pull up and burn any diseased plants, and dig up and remove the soil around their roots, which will harbour spores.

Scab

There are various forms of scab. Potato scab manifests itself by growths on the tubers and is more of a problem where the soil is light. Again, choose disease-resistant varieties and practise good husbandry by clearing away plant debris in the autumn.

Slugs and snails

Slugs and snails eat the leaves of a wide range of plants and also damage soft young stems and even flowers. Control them by placing slug pellets around plants. Alternatively, remove them by hand.

Verticillium

Verticillium wilt is a fungal infection mainly affecting plants grown in the greenhouse and will kill them after a few seasons. At the first sign of the disease – brown markings on the stems and roots – remove and destroy all affected plants; at other stages of the disease, plant foliage wilts and leaves may turn yellow or brown.

Viruses

Viruses are types of diseases that infect a wide range of plants. The most common symptoms are stunted and distorted plants. There is no cure: pull up and burn affected plants.

Weevils

These beetles are easily recognized by their elongated 'snout'. Their larvae are the main problem. Their feeding causes wilting, and invariably death in severe attacks. Use biological control with a pathogenic nematode in late summer.

Wilting leaves

Apart from wilting caused by various pests and diseases, the most common cause is drought. Young plants may never recover, even if watering is carried out. Make sure the soil never dries out, ideally by mulching permanent plants and by watering as necessary.

Woodlice

These pests feed at night and hide in dark places during the day. Physical control is not practical, except to ensure that any plant debris is not left lying around, which will encourage their appearance.

Harvesting, storing and freezing

When to harvest vegetables and how to store them will depend on a number of factors, including the time of year and the type of vegetable. Most vegetables are harvested when fully mature, but a few such as spinach can be cropped repeatedly as a cut-and-come-again crop.

Leafy vegetables, such as Brussels sprouts, are quite hardy and will survive outdoors in temperatures well below freezing point. Many root vegetables, however, have a high moisture content and are easily damaged in winter, even if left in the soil. Exceptions to this are carrots, parsnips and swedes, which are particularly hardy and can be allowed to overwinter in the ground until they are required for consumption.

The main causes of deterioration during storage are moisture loss from the plant tissue (with beetroots and carrots in particular drying out very quickly), or infection and rotting of damaged tissue caused by rough handling when the vegetables were being harvested. Onions and potatoes both tend to bruise particularly easily.

Some vegetables such as onions, chilli peppers, peas, beans and garlic will keep quite well if stored in a dry condition. If they are not to deteriorate, they must be allowed to dehydrate slowly in a cool, dry place. Once dry, store beans and peas in airtight containers. Garlic, chilli peppers and onions can be hung up in an airy place. Any storage area must be frost-free.

Many vegetables also freeze well. These should be blanched before being cooled rapidly and frozen in sealed, airtight boxes or bags.

Ripe vegetables and fruit wait for no one. Always harvest your crops when they are ready and if they cannot be eaten straight away, dry them or freeze them for use later.

It is unlikely that the harvest from a container kitchen garden will be large enough to cause any major storage problems. However, that said, there is every reason to do what you can to ensure that nothing is wasted and that you are able to make the most of your harvest and enjoy all the fruit, vegetables and herbs that you have grown when you want to eat them.

Drying and storing

If you have sufficient space then a number of vegetables, such as onions and potatoes, can be dried off and stored in a cool dry, dark place for several weeks. Carrots and beetroots can also be stored in boxes of sand.

Drying chilli peppers
Bulbous vegetables and chilli peppers should be hung up in an airy, frost-free place to dry.

Harvesting parsnips
Parsnips can be left to overwinter in the soil and dug up as required.

Always harvest young vegetables when they are fresh; many become overripe quickly. Freeze any surplus that you cannot use straight away.

	Crop rotation group	Ease of growing	pH range	Suitable for freezing	Length of growing season	Yield (lb per sq yd)	Tolerates frost
Asparagus	3	M	6.0–7.5	✓	52	3.3	✓
Asparagus peas	1	M	6.0–7.0	✗	7	2.2	✗
Aubergines	3	E	5.5–6.5	✓	9	11.0	✗
Beetroot	3	M	6.5–7.5	✓	8	4.4	✓
Broad beans	1	M	6.5–7.5	✓	20	8.8	✓
Broccoli	2	M	6.0–7.0	✓	8	4.4	✓
Brussels sprouts	2	E	6.0–7.5	✓	8	3.3	✓
Butter beans	1	E	6.5–7.0	✓	10	5.5	✗
Cabbages	2	E	6.5–7.5	✓	10	8.8	✓
Calabrese	2	E	6.5–7.5	✓	8	4.4	✗
Cardoon	3	D	6.5–7.5	✓	52	3.3	✓
Carrots	3	M	6.0–7.5	✓	8–12	4.4	✓
Cauliflowers	2	D	7.0–7.5	✓	8–10	10.0	✓
Celeriac	3	M	6.5–7.5	✓	14	6.6	✓
Celery	3	D	6.5–7.5	✓	14	8.8	✓
Chicory	2	D	6.5–7.5	✗	12	0.9	✓
Chilli pepper	3	M	5.5–6.5	✓	9	3.3	✗
Chinese cabbage	2	E	6.5–7.5	✓	8	3.3	✗
Courgettes and marrows	3	E	5.5–6.5	✓	8	4.4	✗
Cucumber	3	E	5.5–6.5	✗	8	6.6	✗
Endive	2	M	6.5–7.5	✗	12	3.3	✓
Florence fennel	3	D	6.0–7.5	✗	12	6.6	✓
French beans	1	D	6.5–7.5	✗	8	4.4	✗
Garlic	3	M	6.5–7.5	✗	12	4.4	✓
Globe artichoke	3	D	6.5–7.5	✓	52	3.3	✓
Jerusalem artichoke	3	E	6.5–7.5	✗	52	5.5	✓
Kale	2	E	6.5–7.5	✓	10	3.3	✓
Kohl rabi	2	M	6.5–7.0	✓	6	5.5	✓
Lamb's lettuce	2	E	6.5–7.5	✗	8	2.2	✓
Leeks	3	M	6.5–7.5	✓	18–20	3.3	✓
Lettuce	2	E	6.5–7.5	✗	7	2.2	✗
Mangetouts	1	E	6.0–7.0	✗	12	3.3	✗

	Crop rotation group	Ease of growing	pH range	Suitable for freezing	Length of growing season	Yield (lb per sq yd)	Tolerates frost
Mizuna greens	2	E	6.5–7.5	✓	10	3.3	✗
Okra	1	E	6.5–7.0	✗	7	4.4	✗
Onions	3	M	6.5–7.5	✓	10–26	3.3	✗
Pak Choi	2	E	6.5–7.5	✓	✗	3.3	✗
Parsnips	3	M	6.5–7.5	✓	14	3.3	✓
Peas	1	E	6.0–7.0	✓	12	6.6	✗
Peppers	3	E	5.5–6.5	✓	9	3.3	✗
Potatoes	3	E	5.5–6.5	✓	14–22	6.6	✗
Pumpkins	3	E	5.5–6.5	✓	8	6.6	✗
Radishes	3	E	6.0–7.0	✗	3	0.9	✓
Rhubarb	3	E	6.5–7.5	3	8	4.5	✗
Rocket	2	E	6.5–7.5	✗	10	1.1	✓
Salsify	3	M	6.5–7.5	✗	20	3.3	✓
Black salsify	3	M	6.5–7.5	✗	24	4.4	✓
Scarlet runners	1	E	6.5–7.5	✓	10	8.8	✗
Shallots	3	M	6.5–7.5	✓	10–26	3.3	✗
Sorrel	2	E	6.5–7.5	✗	10	1.1	✓
Spinach	2	E	6.5–7.5	✓	6	3.3	✓
Squashes	3	E	5.5–6.5	✗	8	4.4	✗
Swedes	3	E	6.0–7.0	✓	10	4.4	✓
Sweet corn	3	E	6.0–7.0	✓	10	1.1	✗
Sweet peppers	3	M	5.5–6.5	✓	9	3.3	✗
Swiss chard	2	E	6.5–7.5	✗	9	2.2	✓
Tomatoes	3	E	5.5–6.5	✓	10	5.5	✗
Turnips	3	E	6.0–7.0	✓	6–10	3.3	✗

Crop rotation group = 1 Peas and beans, 2 Leaves and flower heads, 3 Roots, stems, and fruiting vegetables

Ease of growing = D difficult, M moderate, E easy

pH Range = Preferred pH

Suitable for freezing = ✓ yes, ✗ no

Length of growing season from outside planting (in weeks)

Yield = pounds per square yard

Tolerates frost =✓ yes, ✗ no

Salad Vegetables

Cichorium endivia
Endive

There are two types of endive: curly-leaved endive, a low-growing plant that looks a bit like curly-headed lettuce, and the broad-leaved Batavian endive, which has broader leaves and makes a more substantial and upright plant. In the kitchen, endive can be used in salads – young, new leaves are best for this – or braised in butter. Traditionally endives are blanched (grown away from light) to make them taste sweeter. Broad-leaved varieties produce attractive white leaves when blanched, although a number of varieties are self-blanching.

Sowing
Sow seed thinly in furrows 13mm (½in) deep and 30cm (12in) apart, from mid-spring onwards.

Cultivation
When the seedlings are 2.5cm (1in) high, thin them to 30cm (12in) apart. Once the plants reach 25cm (10in) across, place an upturned plate on the centre of each to 'blanch' the heart. Water well in dry weather or the plants will bolt.

Harvesting
The plants will be ready to harvest about three weeks after blanching. Cut off the heads just above ground level.

H 20cm (8in)
S 20cm (8in)

16–18°C
(62–64°F)

Direct sunlight

Eruca sativa
Rocket

This tender-looking plant is actually quite hardy and will survive winter temperatures down to just above freezing. The leaves have a strong, tangy flavour which increases in strength when the plant matures or is kept too dry. Rocket can be eaten raw or cooked, and grown as individual plants or harvested regularly as a cut-and-come-again crop. It makes an excellent addition to other leafy vegetables in a mixed salad.

Sowing
Sow seed in succession at three-week intervals from mid-spring to early summer. Sow in broad furrows to create a band of plants about 30cm (12in) wide. If sown in such broad furrows, weeds will be unable to establish themselves owing to the density of the plants.

Cultivation
Keep the plants well watered to promote rapid growth.

Harvesting
Either remove individual leaves from the plants, or cut the seedlings down to about 2.5cm (1in) above ground level, and wait for them to resprout before cutting again.

H 20cm–100cm
(8–39in)

16–18°C
(62–64°F)

Direct sunlight

Lactuca sativa
Lettuces

There are many forms of this annual vegetable, grown for its fresh leaves which are a mainstay of summer salads. For best results, grow several types, such as romaines, cabbage heads and loose-leaf lettuces. Loose-leaf types are less likely to run to seed, and are tolerant of most growing conditions. Leaf colour can vary from pale green to reddish brown, and cultivars such as 'Green Ice' and 'Red Sails' are quite deep rooting, making them ideal for dry soils. Harvesting can begin about 12 weeks after planting.

Sowing
Sow seed thinly in furrows 15mm (½in) deep and 35cm (14in) apart. Sowing at regular intervals from early spring through mid-summer will provide a succession of lettuces from early summer through mid-autumn.

Cultivation
When the seedlings have developed two 'true' leaves, thin to 30cm (12in) apart. In dry weather, keep the plants well watered in the last two weeks before harvesting, when they make the most growth.

Harvesting
Loose-leaf lettuces should be harvested by pulling away the outer rows of leaves from one or two large plants on a regular basis. Cut off the entire heads of other types.

H 20–30cm
(8–12in)

16–18°C
(62–64°F)

Direct sunlight

Lepidium sativum
Cress

Cress is a traditional sprouting crop which many people grow in containers on a windowsill, often on paper. Cress is best grown either in spring or autumn, as it runs to seed quickly and does not relish hot weather; the plants should be kept well watered, especially in dry weather. Land, or American, cress is a good alternative to watercress and has a similar flavour. It may also be cooked. It makes a good filler for the container garden; a few seeds can be sown in situ either to grow in between other vegetables or as a border around the edge of the container.

Sowing
Sow a few seeds in situ throughout the summer. Seed sown in July and August will provide plants in the autumn.

Cultivation
Thin plants to 15cm (6in) apart.

Harvesting
Plants are ready about eight weeks after sowing. Pick leaves as required.

H 5–12cm
(2–5in)

16–18°C
(62–64°F)

Direct sunlight

Rumex acetosa
Sorrel

This versatile plant is an incredibly hardy perennial which is also very easy to grow. The tasty leaves have a sharp flavour and can be used fresh in salads or as a flavouring for soups.

Sorrel will grow on a range of soils, but prefers well-drained yet moisture-retentive, fertile conditions.

Sowing
In autumn or spring, sow seed in furrows 13mm (½in) deep and 30–40cm (12–16in) apart.

Cultivation
Thin the seedlings to 25–30cm (10–12in) apart. Remove any flowers or seed heads as soon as they are spotted – this will preserve the plants' energy for leaf production – and replace the plants themselves every 4–5 years as their productivity declines.

Harvesting
Remove the outer leaves for use as they develop, and new leaves will continue to emerge from the centre of the plant.

H To 90cm (36in)
S 30cm (12in)

10–13°C
(50–55°F)

Direct sunlight

Valeriana locusta

Lamb's Lettuce

Also known as corn salad, this very hardy annual salad crop is grown for its mild-flavoured leaves and will survive winter temperatures down to just above freezing. The erect-growing 'French' cultivars are the hardiest; the 'Dutch' and 'English' forms have a much laxer growth habit, but are more productive. As it takes up very little room, lamb's lettuce is ideal for intercropping between slow-growing or tall vegetable crops. It will do well in most soils and is easy to grow.

Sowing
Sow seed in summer in furrows 15cm (6in) apart, with 2.5cm (1in) between the seeds. For year-round cropping, make an additional sowing in spring.

Cultivation
After germination, thin the seedlings to 10cm (4in) apart, and keep the seedbed well watered until they are about 2.5cm (1in) high.

Harvesting
Either remove individual leaves from the plants, or cut the whole head down to about 2.5cm (1in) above ground level to encourage fresh growth to be made, which can then be cut again for a further crop.

H 15–30cm (6–12in)

10–13°C (50–55°F)

Partial shade

Fruiting Vegetables

Capsicum annuum Grossum Group
Sweet peppers

These annual plants are grown for their characteristic bell-shaped fruits. When ripe, the fruits can be red, yellow, orange and even bluish-black, depending on which cultivars are grown. Sweet peppers prefer a deeply cultivated soil, but also do well in growing bags, pots and troughs; make sure the soil or potting mix is slightly acidic. They require an average temperature of around 21°C (70°F) and fairly high humidity.

Sowing
Sow seed singly in peat pots in mid-spring and germinate at 18°C (64°F). Young plants will be ready to plant out 10 weeks later.

Cultivation
Plant out 75cm (30in) apart. When the plants reach 75cm (30in) high, stake them individually and pinch back the growing point to encourage bushy growth. Spray them with water regularly to keep the humidity high. Once the fruits have started to develop, apply a high-potassium fertilizer every two weeks to encourage them to swell.

Harvesting
Pick the ripe peppers by cutting through the stalk about 2cm (¾in) from the top of the fruit.

H 60–90cm
(24–36in)

18°–21°C
(64–70°F)

Direct sunlight

Capsicum frutescens

Chilli peppers

Also known as hot peppers, these plants are grown for their small, thin, tapering fruits which are green or red when mature, depending on the cultivars grown. The flavour is often very hot, with even the mildest increasing in strength as the fruits mature. The plants can grow up to 60cm (24in) high and 45cm (18in) across, while dwarf cultivars suit pots or growing bags. Chili and cayenne peppers require an average temperature of around 21°C (70°F) and fairly high humidity, so are often grown under protection.

Sowing
Sow seed singly in peat pots in mid-spring and germinate at 18°C (64°F).

Cultivation
Plant out 45cm (18in) apart, and when the plants reach 45cm (18in) high pinch back the growing point to encourage bushy growth. Spray the plants with water regularly to keep the humidity high.

Harvesting
When frost is imminent, pull up the plants and hang them upside down in a frost-free place, where they will continue to ripen and can be used as needed.

H To 60cm (24in)

18°–21°C (64–70°F

Direct sunlight

Lycopersicon esculentum
Tomatoes

Outdoor tomatoes are quite easy to grow and are among the best vegetables for the container gardener. They are attractive plants in flower and fruit, but it has to be said that they do best in relatively warm climates and they are difficult to grow outside unless they can be offered the protection of a south-facing wall and a sheltered position. Tomatoes can be divided into two types, bush and cordon.

The cordon varieties are the most common and if they are to grow successfully they need to be trained up a cane or tied in to wires. Tie the plants in at regular intervals using garden string or raffia and pinch out all the side shoots where the leaf stalks join the stem. This leaves you with one straight stem and a number of trusses of fruit.

When the fourth truss has developed small tomatoes, the growing tip should be pinched out, 'stopped', two leaves above the truss. This allows the tomatoes to develop and ripen properly. If by any chance the summer ends rather earlier than it should and you are left with a large number of green tomatoes, these can be picked and brought inside and will ripen in the warmth of the house. Alternatively, you can use them to make green tomato chutney, a relish prized above many others.

Bush tomatoes are a bit simpler. These varieties grow either as small bushes, as the name implies, or trailing along the ground. They do not require either training or stopping but you do have to cover the ground to prevent

H 1–3m
(3–10ft)

20–25°C
(68–78°F)

Direct sunlight

Lycopersicon esculentum (continued)
Tomatoes

dirt or damage to the fruit, a plastic sheet is the easiest thing to use on a patio, as many of the fruits are at ground level. Dwarf tomatoes, plants that grow little more than 20cm (8in) high, are very suitable for growing in window boxes and small pots but the yield is not large.

The flavour of tomatoes depends on the amount of sunshine they get and the amount of watering and feeding they have received, both of which can reduce the flavour. However, all tomatoes grown in containers or growbags need plenty of watering and feeding as otherwise the yield will be minuscule.

Tomatoes prefer a fertile, well-cultivated soil. They will also grow successfully in pots, troughs and growing bags, but regular watering is essential to produce a good yield of large fruit. Cropping usually starts within 10 weeks of transplanting.

Sowing
For outdoor cultivation, sow seed in late spring. Place individual seeds in 10cm (4in) pots and germinate at 15°C (59°F), hardening the seedlings in a cold frame for 10 days before planting out.

Cultivation
The best growth is achieved at temperatures 20–25°C (68–78°F), and the plants and their fruits can be damaged

Lycopersicon esculentum (continued)
Tomatoes

when temperatures fall below 10°C (50°F), so in colder climates tomatoes are usually grown under glass or in plastic tunnels. Plant out the young plants as the first flowers open.

Plant out bush types first, because they are the hardiest group. Space the plants about 90cm (36in) apart: closer spacings will produce earlier crops, wider spacings a later but heavier yield. The plants can spread along the ground, perhaps on a mulch of straw or plastic. Plant cordon types at a spacing of 75cm (30in) and train them up stakes. Remove any side shoots as they develop, so the plant's energy goes into fruit production. As the fruits develop, apply a high-potassium fertilizer every two weeks to help them swell. When five fruit trusses have formed, remove the main stem at two leaves above this point, to encourage even growth. Then remove the stakes and lay the plants on straw to encourage quicker ripening. To extend the growing season, plastic tunnels can be used to protect the crops.

Harvesting
Pick the fruits as they ripen and remove any leaves covering the fruit to encourage more to do so. If frost threatens in autumn, uproot the plants and hang up in a dry, frost-free place to allow the remaining fruits to ripen.

Solanum melongena

Aubergines

The aubergine is grown for its egg-shaped fruits, which are usually a blackish-purple but may be white-flushed or completely white in cultivars such as 'Easter Egg'. The plants can reach 75cm (30in) high and 60cm (2ft) across and have a deep root system. They therefore prefer a deep, fertile soil, but will also grow well in containers if fertilized and watered generously. Grow in a warm, sheltered spot.

Sowing
Sow seed in small pots in midspring, and germinate at 25°C (78°F). After germination, you will need to lower the temperature to about 16°C (62°F) – if higher than this, the plants will become spindly and prone to collapse.

Cultivation
Plant out as the first flowers start to open, but after there is little risk of frost. Space the plants 75cm (30in) apart, and stake them individually to provide extra support. When the main stem reaches 45cm (18in) high, pinch back the growing point to encourage bushy growth. Once the fruits have started to develop, apply a high-potassium fertilizer every two weeks to help them swell.

Harvesting
Pick the fruits when they are fully swollen, shiny, and firm with a smooth skin. If left too long before picking, the flesh will become bitter.

H 75cm (30in)
S 60cm (24in)

16–25°C
(62–78°F)

Direct sunlight

Squash Vegetables

Cucumis sativus
Cucumber

These tender plants are grown for their characteristic fruits with a high water content. Some cultivars have a bushy, compact habit while others can trail over several yards.

Cucumbers will not tolerate temperatures below 10°C (50°F), so a frost-free environment is essential. The plants will do well in soilless potting mix in growing bags. The fruits will be ready to harvest about eight weeks after sowing.

Sowing
In mid-spring, sow seeds two to a 7.5cm (3in) pot in a temperature of 18–30°C (64–86°F). Thin to one seed per pot.

Cultivation
Once there is little risk of frost and the seedlings are 30cm (12in) high, gradually harden those to be grown outside. Plant at least 40–45cm (16–18in) apart, with 90cm (36in) between rows, to allow lots of light to reach the plants. Train trailing types vertically as cordons up nets or strings at least 2m (6ft) high. Twist support strings around the plants to hold them upright.

Harvesting
The fruits will be ready to harvest by late summer. Cut them from the plant, leaving a stalk of about 2.5cm (1in) on each fruit.

H 1.8–2.4m (6–8ft)

16–18°C (62–64°F)

Direct sunlight

Cynara cardunculus Scolymus Group

Globe artichokes

These large, bushy perennials are grown for their greenish-purple flower bracts and have a cropping life of three years.

Sowing

Sow seed 2.5cm (1in) deep in a seedbed in early spring in rows 30cm (12in) apart with 10cm (4in) between the seeds. Transplant into the cropping site in early summer. These seedlings will be variable, however, so division of named varieties is preferable.

Cultivation

Before planting, spread a 10cm (4in) layer of well-rotted manure and dig the ground to one spade's depth. Plant young side shoots 5cm (2in) deep and 90cm (36in) apart all around, and trim back the shoots by half their length to prevent wilting. After planting, spread a 10cm (4in) layer of manure around the plants to reduce weeds and moisture loss. Protect over winter with a layer of straw, until early spring, when each plant will produce two or three shoots to bear the flower heads.

Harvesting

From early summer to early autumn, depending on the age of the plants, each stem will carry one primary flower head and several secondary ones. These should be cut when they are about 10cm (4in) across, removing each one with a 10cm (4in) section of stem.

H 1.2–2.4m
(4–8ft)

16–25°C
(62–78°F)

Direct sunlight

Cucurbita pepo
Courgettes and marrows

Another member of the cucumber family, courgettes are a widely grown favourite summer vegetable. Those grown in the garden are far better to eat than any bought in a shop. The best courgettes to grow are the compact bush varieties; provided the fruits are harvested regularly, they will continue to produce fruit over a long period.

Grown for their long, cylindrical fruits, courgettes come in a range of colours from white, through grey, to deep green; some cultivars, such as 'Spineless Beauty', are a mixture of green and cream-white stripes. The fruits, with their smooth, shiny skin, will be ready to harvest about 6–8 weeks after sowing.

Although any variety of these immature squashes can be eaten when young, it is best to choose a modern hybrid variety of courgette. Numerous new cultivars have been introduced, with fruit colours ranging from the dark green of 'Embassy', through lighter shades, to the yellow of 'Gold Rush'.

Sowing
In spring, soak the seeds overnight and then sow individually in 7.5cm (3in) peat pots at a temperature of 15°C (59°F).

H To 90cm (36in)
S To 90cm (36in)

16–18°C
(62–64°F)

Direct sunlight

Cucurbita pepo (continued)
Courgettes and marrows

Cultivation
Harden off the young plants before planting out. Plant bush types 90cm (36in) apart; trailing cultivars will need at least 2m (6ft) all around unless trained vertically, when they can be planted at the same spacing as bush types. Immediately after planting out, make sure that the plants are protected from overnight frost.

Each plant needs a minimum of 13.5 litres (3 gallons) of water per week. Mulch with a layer of organic matter at least 10cm (4in) deep, to retain soil moisture. Cut away any leaves shading the fruits. As the fruits start to swell, remove any male flowers close by to prevent the fruits developing a bitter taste.

Harvesting
Although they can grow much larger, courgettes are usually harvested when the fruits are 10–15cm (4–6in) long. Regular picking encourages the production of further flowers and fruits. Towards the end of the season allow one or two fruits to mature into marrows. These can then be stored for several months in an airy, frost-free environment. Remember to avoid leaving marrows too long or they will become tough. Pick when the fruits are 25cm (10in) long – if your thumbnail goes in easily, they are ready.

Cucurbita maxima, C. moschata

Squashes and pumpkins

Pumpkins belong to the same family as marrows and courgettes, and come in a wide range of shapes, sizes and colours. They are not suitable for a patio garden with limited room, but there is no doubt that a traditional orange pumpkin is a triumph for the gardener at Hallowe'en.

These tender plants are grown for their unusual fruits, which vary tremendously in shape and size – from the large, orange fruits of the traditional Hallowe'en pumpkin to the curved shape of crookneck and the distinctive 'Turk's turban' squash. They can weigh up to 227kg (500lb) each and come in a range of colours from yellow to grey-green.

Squashes, crooknecks and pumpkins grow best in a warm, sheltered position and are generally ready to harvest seven weeks after sowing. 'Gold Bar' is a useful cultivar, producing fruits weighing up to 1kg (2lb). 'Park's' crookneck has fewer spines so is less prickly to harvest.

Sowing
In mid- to late spring, soak the seeds overnight in cold water and then sow individually in 7.5cm (3in) pots. Raise at 12–14°C (54–57°F).

Cultivation
Harden off the young plants for 2–3 weeks before planting out once there is little risk of frost. However, if frost is forecast, make sure that the plants are protected with

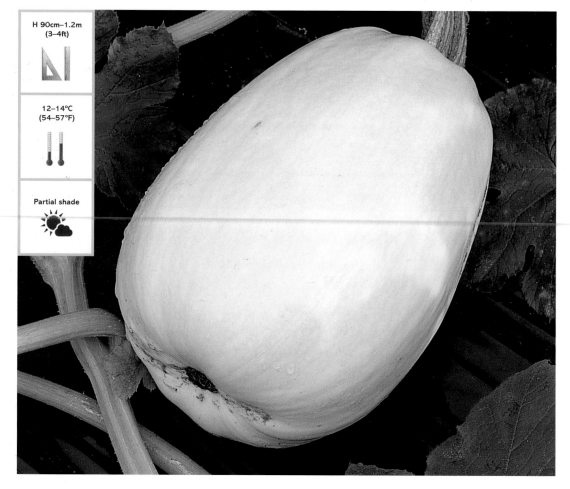

H 90cm–1.2m
(3–4ft)

12–14°C
(54–57°F)

Partial shade

Cucurbita maxima, C. moschata (continued)

Squashes and pumpkins

fleece. Plant bush types 90cm (36in) apart; trailing cultivars need at least 2m (6ft) all around.

Each plant requires a minimum of 13.5 litres (3 gallons) of water per week. Mulch with a layer of organic matter at least 10cm (4in) deep, to retain soil moisture. Cut away any leaves that shade the fruits. As the fruits start to swell, remove any male flowers that are close by to prevent the fruits developing a bitter taste.

Harvesting

Although they can grow much larger, the fruits are usually harvested when 20–25cm (8–10in) across, or when the foliage starts to turn yellow and the fruit stems start to crack. This is often just before the first hard frost occurs. After severing the fruit from the parent plant, dry it for about 10 days outdoors, using the warmth of the sun to improve storage quality. Then place the fruit in a string or netting bag, and hang it in an airy, frost-free place at a temperature of 10°C (50°F) for up to six months.

Protecting seedlings

Inverted jam jars can be used to protect young plants.

Ripening pumpkins

Lay black plastic sheeting underneath ripening pumpkins, crooknecks and other squashes to keep them off the ground.

Zea mays

Sweet corn

Sweetcorn is the modern descendant of a very ancient plant native to Central America. Not surprisingly, it is more at home in a Mediterranean climate than in a cool temperate one, but given purpose-bred varieties and a good summer, there is every chance of success in reasonably mild regions. The site should be open and must receive plenty of sun. A soil well supplied with garden compost or manure and sufficient lime to correct strong acidity is also necessary. In order to get good results, sweetcorn must have a long growing season. Modern varieties will be ready for picking about four months after sowing. However, you must balance this

with having the plants inside and protected while there is still a risk of spring frosts. Sow the seeds, therefore, in a greenhouse in mid-spring or in a cold frame from mid- to late spring. Plant the seedlings out when the risk of frost is over. If you do not have either a greenhouse or cold frame, you can sow the seeds where the plants are to grow outdoors in late spring or early summer. Once established, keep weeds at bay to avoid competition. When hoeing, be careful not to disturb, and certainly not damage, the surface roots; these are important feeding roots as well as the plant's main support. Provide plenty of water in dry weather. Do not plant traditional and

H To 2.5m (8ft)

16–25°C (62–78°F)

Direct sunlight

Zea mays (continued)
Sweet corn

supersweet varieties together, as cross-pollination can affect the quality of the supersweets.

Sowing
Sow seed under protection, with three seeds to a 7.5cm (3in) pot. Outdoors, sow seed from mid-spring in a seedbed in a warm, sheltered spot.

Cultivation
Sweet corn relies on the wind to pollinate the plants. To facilitate this, plant in square or rectangular, 6-row blocks, with the plants spaced 35cm (14in) apart all around.

Before transplanting pot-grown seedlings, cover the planting area with black plastic to warm the soil. When the seedlings are 15–20cm (6–8in) high, insert the young plants into the soil through the plastic and shelter them from wind for the first week after planting. Most of the plants will produce four or five cobs – to get large cobs, water the plants well as the cobs are developing.

Harvesting
The cobs will be ready to harvest from mid-summer to mid-autumn. When the tassel ('silk') at the top of the cob starts to turn brown, snap the cob from the main stem.

Pod and Seed Vegetables

Abelmoschus esculentus

Okra

Grown for its elegant, edible pods, okra is nicknamed lady's finger because of its resemblance in shape. This tender vegetable must have as long a growing season as possible, because it will take at least seven weeks from sowing until harvesting the pods.

Sowing
In midspring, sow three seeds per 7.5cm (3in) pot at a temperature of 18–24°C (65–75°F). Thin the two smallest seedlings from each pot.

Cultivation
The plants should be 15–20cm (6–8in) high before they are planted out, usually from early summer onwards, once there is little risk of frost. Before planting, cover the planting area with black plastic for at least three weeks to warm the soil, and insert the young plants into the soil through the plastic. Space them at 35cm (14in) all around to encourage strong, bushy plants. They must be sheltered from winds for the first week after being planted.

Harvesting
From mid-summer until early autumn, harvest the pods while they are still immature and before the seeds have developed fully. Cut them from the stem with a sharp knife. Harvest the pods as they form, to encourage the plant to produce more.

H 60–90cm
(24–36in)

16–18°C
(62–64°F)

Direct sunlight

Pisum sativum

Peas

Garden peas are grown for their sweet-tasting, edible seeds, which are produced in green or (in a few cultivars) purple pods. The peas are generally round with a wrinkled or smooth skin, and can be eaten fresh – either cooked, or raw in salads – or dried and stored for use later.

   The time from sowing to harvesting varies with each type. If you sow early crop peas in mid-spring, they will be ready to harvest 12 weeks later in mid-summer. Crops of maincrop cultivars will be ready to harvest about 10–12 weeks after sowing.

Sowing

Sow seed in flat-bottomed furrows 3–5cm (1–2in) deep. String foil across the rows to deter birds from taking the seeds or attacking the seedlings.

Cultivation

Keep the plants well watered from soon after flowering starts.

Harvesting

Start harvesting the pods when they are well developed but before they become too tightly packed with peas. Keep picking regularly to encourage further flowering.

H 45cm–1.5m
(18in–5ft)

16–18°C
(62–64°F)

Partial shade

Pisum sativum var. *macrocarpon*

Mangetouts

Also known as snow peas, mangetouts are grown for their delicate, sweet-tasting pods, which are eaten young and whole. Alternatively, mangetouts can be harvested later, in the same way as garden peas. They will be ready to harvest eight weeks after sowing.

Sowing
Sow seeds from mid-spring onwards at three-week intervals to provide a succession of crops throughout the summer. Sow in flat-bottomed furrows 4cm (1½in) wide and 15cm (6in) apart, with 10cm (4in) between the seeds. For cropping purposes, sow in blocks of three furrows, which can be separated from the next block by a 45cm (18in) path.

Cultivation
The crop is larger when the plants are supported by stakes, sticks, or plastic or wire mesh. With the three-row system, arrange the support over the rows in a tent-like structure, about 45–60cm (18–24in) tall.

Harvesting
The perfect stage for picking is when the peas are just visibly swelling in the pods. Harvest the pods by tugging them gently from the stem.

H 90cm–2m
(3–6ft)

13–18°C
(55–64°F)

Partial shade

Phaseolus coccineus

Scarlet runners

These easy-to-grow vines were originally introduced as ornamentals. Today, scarlet runners are grown mainly for their long, edible pods which are produced prolifically until the first frost.

Grown as annuals, scarlet runners require a sturdy support system, because they can reach heights of 2.5–3m (8–10ft) in their growing season of 10 weeks.

Sowing
Sow seeds in late spring or early summer – scarlet runners grow better in warm soil. Using a dibble, spot-sow 5cm (2in) deep in a double row spaced 60cm (2ft) apart and with 15cm (6in) between the seeds, to give the plants plenty of room as they grow. In colder areas, sow the

beans indoors, two or three to a 15cm (6in) pot. Transplant when about 10cm (4in) tall.

Cultivation
Insert the supports when the plants are about 15cm (6in) high, just as the twining stem starts to develop in the tip of the plant. Water the roots well from soon after flowering and continue throughout the harvesting period.

Harvesting
The pods will be ready for picking from mid-summer onwards and harvesting can continue until the first frost, when the plants are killed.

H 2.5–3m
(8–10ft)

16–18°C
(62–64°F)

Direct sunlight

Phaseolus lunatus

Butter beans

Also known as the 'lima bean', this plant is grown for its large, white seeds, although the young pods can be eaten whole about six weeks after sowing. The plants prefer a warm climate and a well-drained soil.

There are both bush and pole forms of the lima bean – the latter being useful in small gardens where space is at a premium. The beans will be ready to harvest 10 weeks after sowing.

Sowing

Sow seeds from late spring onwards 7.5cm (3in) deep and 30–45cm (12–18in) apart. Allow 75cm (30in) between the rows for pole cultivars, slightly less for bush forms.

Cultivation

Provide pole cultivars with stakes at least 1.8m (6ft) tall for adequate support. Once the plants reach 30cm (12in) high, supply a brand-name liquid fertilizer at two-week intervals to ensure growth, but stop fertilizing when the plants start to flower.

Harvesting

The beans will be ready to harvest when the swollen seeds are visible in the pods. Pull pods gently to prevent damage to the stems.

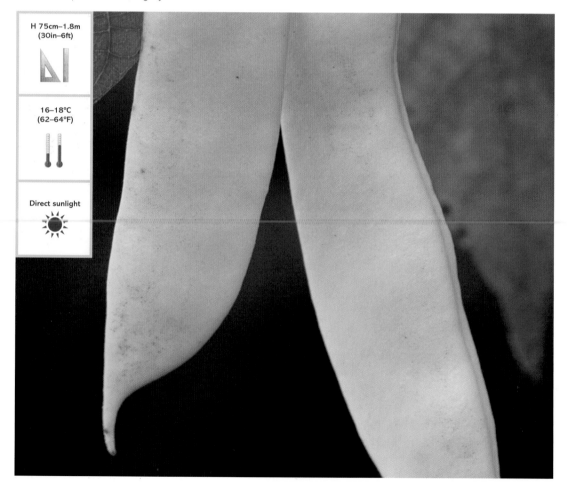

H 75cm–1.8m
(30in–6ft)

16–18°C
(62–64°F)

Direct sunlight

Phaseolus vulgaris

French beans

Also known as green beans, French beans are grown for their curved, green pods which are eaten whole and for their partially developed seeds. Bush forms will grow 40–45cm (16–18in) high and 30–45cm (12–18in) wide. Pole cultivars can be grown up supports. Harvest eight weeks after sowing.

Sowing

Sow seeds at three-week intervals from late spring until mid-summer. Plant 5cm (2in) deep in double rows spaced 20cm (8in) apart, with about 15cm (6in) between seeds. Stagger them to give plenty of room.

Cultivation

Keep plants well watered once flowering starts to increase the crop and delay the onset of stringiness.

Harvesting

Pick regularly once the pods are about 10cm (4in) long and will snap cleanly in half.

Weather protection

A late crop of green beans should be protected by glass.

H 40–45cm (16–18in)
S 30–45cm (12–18in)

16–18°C (62–64°F)

Partial shade

Psophocarpus tetragonolobus

Asparagus peas

Asparagus peas are grown for their decorative, scarlet to chocolate-brown flowers, delicate bluish-green foliage, and triangular, 'winged' pods that have an asparagus-like flavour. They are eaten whole. The pods will be ready for picking about eight weeks after sowing. However, do not expect large quantities of pods: even a heavy yield will be only about half that of garden peas. These plants grow best in a sunny position in a well-drained soil.

Sowing

Sow seed in mid- to late spring, in furrows about 3cm (1in) deep and 30cm (12in) apart, with about 30cm (12in) between the seeds.

Cultivation

Support the plants with stakes, sticks or plastic or wire mesh, or they will produce very few pods. Protection from birds is essential: suspending nets on stakes above the crop is the best method.

Harvesting

The pods are ready for picking from mid-summer until early autumn. For the best flavour, harvest the pods while still immature and 3–5cm (1–2in) long. Pick regularly to encourage further flowering and the production of more pods.

H 45cm (18in)
S 60cm (24in)

16–18°C
(62–64°F)

Direct sunlight

Vicia faba

Broad beans

Broad beans are very hardy plants, and will give a good crop with very little care and attention. They are grown mainly for their edible, greenish-white seeds, which develop inside thick, hairy pods, but the immature pods can be eaten when about 10cm (4in) long and the young shoots are also tasty. Those sown in autumn will take up to 20 weeks to harvest; spring-sown crops are ready in 12 weeks.

Sowing

Seeds germinate better at lower temperature so sow in late autumn (this will discourage aphid, to which broad beans are prone, since the plants will flower before the aphids are out in force) or in early spring. Using a dibble, spot-sow 5cm (2in) deep in a double row spaced at 30cm (12in) apart, with 25cm (10in) between the seeds to give plenty of room.

Cultivation

Most cultivars need support, and well-branched twigs 45cm (18in) tall will allow the plants to grow up through them. Water the plants well once flowering starts and throughout harvest-time.

Harvesting

If you sow in autumn and spring, you should have broad beans for picking from late spring to mid-autumn.

H 50cm–1.8m
(20in–6ft)

16–18°C
(62–64°F)

Partial shade

85

Leafy Vegetables

Beta vulgaris Cicla Group

Swiss chard

This hardy vegetable is grown for its large, glossy, succulent leaves, which can be up to 45cm (18in) long and 20cm (8in) wide. The brightly coloured leaf stalks are red or white, and the leaves range in colour from the deep green of 'Fordhook Giant' to the lime-green of 'Lucullus' or copper-green of 'Rhubarb Chard'. The best-known is red-stemmed Swiss chard, also known as ruby chard, which is easy to grow but prone to bolting, especially in hot, dry weather. Swiss chard prefers a fertile, well-drained but moisture-retentive soil.

Sowing

Incorporate plenty of organic matter into the soil before sowing. Sow seed for new plants at any time from early spring to mid-summer into furrows 2cm (¾in) deep and 45 cm (18in) apart, with 15cm (6in) between the seeds.

Cultivation

When the seedlings are about 5cm (2in) high, thin them to 30cm (12in) apart – as a long-term crop, the plants need plenty of room or mildew may attack them. For cut-and-come-again crops, thin to 7.5cm (3in) apart.

Harvesting

Harvest the plants grown at wider spacings by cutting off the outer leaves at soil level.

H 90cm–2m
(3–6ft)

16–18°C
(62–64°F)

Direct sunlight

Brassica oleracea Capitata Group

Cabbages

The tightly packed leaves and growing point of the cabbage plant are often referred to as the 'head' or 'heart', and this varies in size and shape – from round, through pointed to almost flat – according to type and cultivar. Growing a selection of the many types on offer makes it possible to have fresh cabbage available to eat year-round, harvesting even through quite severe winter conditions.

All types of cabbage are cultivated in much the same way, with the timing of sowing and planting varying according to the season, the cultivars chosen, and the time taken to reach maturity. The soil should be slightly alkaline to discourage a disease called club root, so apply lime if necessary.

Sowing

Sow seed thinly 2cm (¾in) deep in a well-prepared seedbed outdoors from mid- to late spring through to mid-summer, depending on the cabbage type. For many of the sowings, watering may be required to make sure the seedlings keep growing rapidly. If cabbages dry out, they will produce 'hearts' too easily or 'bolt' to produce seed.

Cultivation

Transplant the seedlings. Firm the soil well by treading it down before planting to encourage a strong root system which will support the plants. Plant out spring cabbages at a spacing of 30cm (12in) all around, summer and autumn

H 30–45cm
(12–18in)

16–18°C
(62–64°F)

Direct sunlight

Brassica oleracea Capitata Group (continued)

Cabbages

types at 40 x 45cm (16 x 18in) and hardy winter cabbages at a spacing of 50 x 50cm (20 x 20in) apart.

Harvesting
When the cabbage has developed a good-sized, solid heart, it is ready for harvesting. Using a sharp knife, cut through the main stem to remove the entire heart and a few outer leaves, leaving the oldest leaves and the stem in the soil.

How to transplant brassicas
When the seedlings have three or four 'true' leaves, they are ready for transplanting into rows 30cm (12in) apart, with 45cm (18in) between the plants.

This crop matures quite rapidly and can take as little as 10 weeks from germination to harvest. However, because it is shallow rooted it is very important to keep the plants well watered.

1 Before transplanting, check that the growing point on a young plant is undamaged.

2 Embed the seedling to the depth of the lowest 'true' leaves to stabilize the plants.

3 The plant is firmly enough planted only if a leaf snaps or tears when tugged.

Brassica oleracea Gemmifera Group

Brussels sprouts

These very hardy vegetables are grown for their edible flower buds, which form small, tight, 'cabbagelike' sprouts in the leaf joints of the plant's main stem. Tall cultivars are ideal if space is limited, since they can be grown close together and produce a good 'vertical' crop. The soil for Brussels sprouts should be slightly alkaline to discourage club root disease, so apply lime if necessary. They take about 12 weeks from sowing to harvesting.

Sowing

Sow seed thinly into a seedbed outdoors in mid- to late spring. Some watering may be required to make sure that the seedlings keep growing rapidly.

Cultivation

Firm the soil well by treading it down before planting to encourage a strong root system which will hold the plants erect. When the seedlings have developed three or four 'true' leaves, transplant them into their cropping site with the rows 60cm (24in) apart and 60cm (24in) between the plants, firming each plant well into the soil.

Harvesting

The sprouts will be ready to harvest from early autumn though to mid-spring, depending on the cultivar. To pick, pull the individual sprouts downwards so that they snap from the stem.

H 60cm–1.2m
(2–4ft)

15–18°C
(59–64°F)

Direct sunlight

Brassica oleracea Acephala Group

Kale

This is the hardiest of annual winter vegetables. The soil for kale should be slightly alkaline to discourage club root, so apply lime if necessary.

Sowing

Sow seed in late spring outdoors in a seedbed. You may need to protect the seedlings against birds.

Cultivation

When the seedlings have developed four 'true' leaves, transplant them into their cropping site, spacing the rows about 60cm (24in) apart, with 45cm (18in) between the plants. Water well until established.

Harvesting

Harvest on a cut-and-come-again basis from mid-autumn to mid-spring by snapping off young leaves from all the plants. This will prevent any leaves from maturing and becoming tough and 'stringy'.

Hoeing between rows

Hoeing between kale plants controls weeds as they emerge.

H 30–60cm
(12–24in)

10–13°C
(50–55°F)

Partial shade

Brassica rapa Chinensis Group

Chinese cabbage

This annual plant is grown for its crisp, delicately flavoured leaves with white mid-ribs which are used fresh in salads. It is relatively fast growing and may be ready to harvest as little as eight weeks from germination.

Chinese cabbage resents root disturbance and is usually raised in pots. Transplant seedlings when three 'true' leaves are about 5cm (2in) high.

Sowing

Sow seed individually in plastic or peat pots 7.5cm (3in) square in mid-summer. They need temperatures of 20–25°C (68–78°F) to germinate, so raise in a cold frame or greenhouse.

Cultivation

When the seedlings have developed four 'true' leaves, transplant outdoors into rows about 30cm (12in) apart, with 45cm (18in) between the plants. Chinese cabbage is shallow rooted, and the plants must be kept well watered.

Harvesting

Starting in late summer, harvesting can last for up to 14 weeks with successional sowings. Cut through the stem just above ground level to remove the heart. The remaining stalk will often sprout clusters of new leaves, which can be harvested later on.

H 30–45cm
(12–18in)

20–25°C
(68–78°F)

Direct sunlight

Brassica oleracea Italica Group

Purple sprouting broccoli

Grown for its edible flower heads, which are harvested while in tight bud, purple sprouting broccoli is a very hardy, biennial, winter vegetable. There are both white- and purple-flowered forms. The soil for broccoli should be slightly alkaline in order to discourage club root, so apply lime if necessary.

Sowing
Sow seeds individually in 5cm (2in) square plastic or peat pots, in a cold frame or unheated greenhouse in spring.

Cultivation
Plant out in early summer with 60cm (24in) between the plants all around. Water is essential to produce a good crop, the critical time being the first month after sowing. Surround young stems with extra soil to reduce windrock.

Harvesting
Broccoli can be harvested from late winter until late spring and has a natural cut-and-come-again habit. Cut the central spike first, before the flowers start to open; side shoots will also try to flower and these smaller spikes can be cut later.

H To 60cm (24in)
S To 30cm (12in)

16–18°C
(62–64°F)

Direct sunlight

Brassica oleracea Botrytis Group

Cauliflowers

Cauliflowers are grown for their edible flower heads, which are harvested while they are in tight bud. Cauliflowers can be available for most of the year, and certainly from early spring through to mid-winter. Autumn- and spring-heading cauliflowers are the easiest to grow, often producing curds (immature flower heads) up to 30cm (12in) across. They will be ready to harvest in 8–10 weeks.

Cauliflowers are often judged on the whiteness and lack of blemishes on their curds. There are also forms with green and purple heads, which have an outstanding flavour.

Cauliflowers are among the most difficult vegetables to grow well. They need plenty of water to ensure rapid growth and resent root disturbance, so should be transplanted as young as possible, certainly within six weeks of germination. If transplanted too late or allowed to dry out at this stage, they may produce small, premature, tight curds which are tough and woody.

The soil for cauliflowers should be slightly alkaline to discourage club root and because acidic soils can promote some nutrient deficiencies, resulting in poor curds. (Apply lime if necessary.)

Sowing

Sow seeds individually in plastic or peat pots 7.5cm (3in) square, and raise in a cold frame or unheated greenhouse.

H To 60cm (24in)
S To 60cm (24in)

16–18°C
(62–64°F)

Direct sunlight

Brassica oleracea Botrytis Group (continued)

Cauliflowers

Sow early-summer cauliflowers in mid-autumn for harvesting the following spring; autumn cauliflowers in late spring for harvesting in autumn; winter cauliflowers in late spring for harvesting the following winter; and sow spring cauliflowers in late spring for harvesting in early spring the following year.

Cultivation

When the seedlings have developed four 'true' leaves, they are ready for transplanting to their cropping site. Spacing depends on the time of year; generally, the later the planting, the larger the cauliflower will grow and the greater the space needed for each plant. Early-summer cauliflowers, for example, should be planted at a spacing of 60 x 45cm (24 x 18in), winter cauliflowers at 75cm (30in) all around.

Harvesting

When the covering leaves start to open and show the enclosed curd beneath, the cauliflower is ready to harvest. Using a sharp knife, cut through the main stem to remove the complete curd, together with a row of leaves around it to protect the curd from damage and marking.

Brassica oleracea Italica Group

Broccoli/Calabrese

Grown as an annual for its edible flower heads, broccoli (also called calabrese) is similar to sprouting broccoli but less hardy, although it can be harvested in early spring if grown under protection. Many cultivars will mature within eight weeks of sowing.

Well-grown broccoli is tasty eaten fresh and ideal for freezing, the drawback being that the plant is very susceptible to mealy aphids, attracted to the flower spikes.

The soil for broccoli should be slightly alkaline in order to discourage club root, so apply lime if necessary. Broccoli resents root disturbance and often responds to transplanting by prematurely producing small, tight heads which can be tough and woody.

Sowing
Sow seed thinly in furrows 2.5cm (1in) deep and about 30cm (12in) apart, sowing three seeds 13 mm (½in) apart in spots at 20cm (8in) intervals. Alternatively, sow seeds individually into 5cm (2in) diameter plastic or peat pots in a cold frame or unheated greenhouse if cold weather demands an earlier start.

Cultivation
When the seedlings have developed three 'true' leaves, thin them to leave only the strongest and healthiest seedling at each spot. Transplant pot-grown seedlings at this point. Watering is essential to keep the plants growing rapidly

H To 60cm (24in)
S To 30cm (12in)

16–18°C
(62–64°F)

Direct sunlight

Brassica oleracea Italica Group (continued)
Broccoli

and to produce a good crop – critical times are the first month after sowing and the three-week period just before cropping commences.

Harvesting
The main cropping season is from early summer to mid-autumn, but harvesting can continue until the plants are damaged by the first frost, before the flowers (usually yellow) start to open. The slightly smaller spikes produced by the side shoots can be cut later. Main-season plantings will often yield up to four or five cuttings before the plants are discarded. (They make useful compost.)

Applying lime
Lime can be applied at any time of year to raise the soil's pH but must be added alone, at least two to three months after manuring, or one month after fertilizing the soil. This is because lime and nitrogen react to release ammonia, which can harm plants.

If lime is used first however, fertilizers and manures can be added just one month later. It is also simpler to add lime before crops are sown or transplanted into the site. If lime is applied too often, plants may show signs of nutrient deficiency. Bear in mind that it is easier to raise the soil pH than it is to lower it.

Brassica rapa var. nipposinica

Mizuna greens

Grow Mizuna greens as a cut-and-come-again crop. This plant will benefit from some protection from the sun in high summer.

Sowing

Sow thinly in drills from mid-summer, thinning out to about 15cm (6in) apart. Sow under cover in autumn for a winter crop.

Cultivation

Keep weed-free and well-watered. Use a net to protect Mizuna greens from pests.

Harvesting

Ready in three weeks. Pick the leaves as needed, leaving the plant in the ground to resprout.

H 27cm (11in)
S 30cm (12in)

16–18°C
(62–64°F)

Partial shade

Brassica rapa var. chinensis

Pak Choi

Closely related to the Chinese cabbage, all parts of the Pak Choi plant can be eaten. Varieties differ in height from 8–10cm (3–4in) to 45cm (18in). Look for bolt-resistant varieties.

Sowing

Sow seeds in situ 1cm (½in) deep, in rows 30cm (12in) apart, every few weeks for a continuous crop. Thin according to the size desired: small, 15cm (6in) apart; medium 18cm (7in) apart; large 35cm (14in) apart. Sow under cover in autumn for a winter crop.

Cultivation

Keep weed-free and water well.

Harvesting

Ready in three weeks. Pick the leaves as needed, leaving the plant in the ground to resprout.

H 30–45cm (12–18in)

20–25°C (68–78°F)

Direct sunlight

Spinacia oleracea

Spinach

This reasonably hardy vegetable is renowned for its strongly flavoured, dark green leaves, which are rich in iron and vitamins.

Spinach prefers a well-drained but moisture-retentive, fertile soil which is high in nitrogen. It will tolerate light shade. Although a perennial, it is best grown as an annual in order to produce the most vigorous leaves. The plants will often 'bolt' (run to seed) and develop seed in the first year, especially during periods of hot, dry weather.

Spinach is usually ready for eating about six weeks after sowing. Individual leaves can be removed, or the whole plant cut back to produce new leaves for cut-and-come-again harvesting.

Sowing
For a continuous supply, sow seed thinly in furrows at three-week intervals from early spring to mid-summer.

Cultivation
When the seedlings are 2.5cm (1in) high, thin them to 15cm (6in) apart. For cut-and-come-again crops, thin to 5cm (2in).

Harvesting
Harvest plants grown at wide spacings by cutting off the outer leaves at ground level.

H 30cm (12in)
S 30cm (12in)

16–18°C
(62–64°F)

Direct sunlight

Stem Vegetables

Allium porrum

Leeks

Like onions, you can sow leeks either in a heated greenhouse in mid- to late winter or outside in the early to mid-spring. In either event, plant the seedlings outside in their final position when they are about as thick as pencils.

To grow leeks plant out the seedlings in early to mid-summer. Make holes 15cm (6in) deep and 15cm (6in) apart and, having trimmed the roots back to about 1.25cm (½in) long, drop a plant into each hole. No firming in is needed, you merely pour water into the hole. This covers the roots with soil and ensures that the little plants will flourish.

One of the hardiest of winter vegetables, leeks have a long cropping season, from early autumn, through winter, and into late spring of the following year.

Sowing
In late spring sow seed thinly, 3cm (1in) apart, in drills 3cm (1in) deep and 30cm (12in) apart.

Cultivation
Transplant seedlings when they are 20cm (8in) high, the main planting season being mid-summer. Incorporate a dressing of high-nitrogen fertilizer into the soil surface before planting.

Harvesting
Harvest leeks when their leaves start to hang down, from early autumn onwards, by lifting them with a garden fork.

H 60cm (24in)
S 20cm (8in)

16–18°C
(62–64°F)

Direct sunlight

Apium graveolens
Celery

Celery is grown for its crisp, blanched leaf stalks, which can be white, pink or red. Newer, self-blanching forms are easier to grow since they do not need to be artificially blanched. Celery needs a sunny, open site with deep, stone-free, well-drained, fertile soil that has had plenty of organic matter incorporated. To prevent plants from 'bolting' or producing stringy leaf stalks, keep them growing steadily.

Sowing
Sow seed in trays or peat pots under protection from early to late spring. Place seed on the surface of the potting mix. Self-blanching celery needs warmth to germinate – the temperature should be above 10°C (50°F).

Cultivation
About eight weeks after sowing, harden the seedlings in a cold frame. From late spring on, when the plants have developed five to six 'true' leaves, plant them out. Celery needs plenty of water to grow quickly and remain crisp.

Harvesting
Harvesting for trench celery can begin in late autumn, when the leaf stalks are crunchy to eat; the pink and red forms are the hardiest and will be harvested last. Dig out the soil around each plant, lift the celery, then cut off the head and roots. Self-blanching celery can be harvested from mid-summer onwards. Celery can be left in the ground over winter.

H 60cm (24in)
S 15cm (6in)

16–18°C
(62–64°F)

Direct sunlight

Apium graveolens Rapaceum Group
Celeriac

This vegetable is grown for its celery-flavoured, swollen stem, which takes six months to mature after sowing. It can be cooked or used raw.

Grow celeriac in a sunny, open site in free-draining soil. It may eventually reach 75cm (30in) high.

Sowing
Sow seed in trays or modules under protection, at a temperature of 16°C (61°F) from early spring onwards for a continuous supply.

Cultivation
About six weeks after sowing, harden off the seedlings in a cold frame. Plant them out in rows 30cm (12in) apart, with 40cm (16in) between the plants, with the stems just visible on the soil surface. In late autumn, remove the outer leaves to encourage the stems to swell, and mulch with straw to protect from severe frost.

Harvesting
Harvest celeriac from late summer until the following spring, digging up the plants with a garden fork. However, plants will survive in the ground in most sites.

H 60cm (24in)
S 15cm (6in)

16–18°C
(62–64°F)

Direct sunlight

Asparagus officinalis

Asparagus

This herbaceous perennial can produce crops of its delicious shoots ('spears') for up to 25 years, so requires a permanent site.

Asparagus prefers deep, fertile, well-drained soil which has had plenty of organic matter incorporated into it 2–3 months before planting. In spring, before the spears emerge, the soil is often top-dressed with salt, which controls weeds but does not harm the crop.

Cultivation

Asparagus plants grown from seed give a variable crop, so it is best to purchase one-year-old asparagus crowns. Plant crowns in early spring, 10–15cm (4–6in) deep and 45cm

(18in) apart, in ridge-bottomed trenches 30cm (12in) apart. Cut down and remove all top-growth in late autumn as it turns yellow.

Harvesting

After the asparagus bed has been established for 1–2 years, you can then harvest the spears. Harvesting usually begins in mid-spring and lasts for eight weeks. When the spears are 15cm (6in) high, cut them with a sharp knife, slicing through the stem 2–3cm (1–1½in) below soil level. Keep the cut spears covered to prevent them drying out.

H 1.5m (5ft)
S 90cm (36in)

16–18°C
(62–64°F)

Direct sunlight

Cynara cardunculus

Cardoon

Once its blanched stems were a popular vegetable, but now the cardoon is more often grown as a border plant for its dramatic foliage and thistle-like flowers. It grows to 1.8m (6ft).

Sowing

In late spring, sow three seeds per module under glass, thin to the strongest and plant out once all danger of frosts has passed. Or, station-sow in situ in early summer: sow three seeds 5cm (2in) deep in each station, leaving 60cm (24in) between stations. Thin out to the strongest.

Cultivation

Keep weed-free and well-watered in dry conditions. Feed weekly with a liquid fertilizer. Stake when the plant has grown to about 30cm (12in) high. Blanch in late summer or early autumn: pull the stems loosely together and tie collars of newspaper or brown paper around the stems. Earth up the base and leave for four weeks.

Harvesting

Ready in six months. Dig up the plant and cut away the leaves and roots. Divide the roots, snip off the offsets and plant up for next year.

H 1.8m (6ft)
S 90cm (36in)

16–18°C
(62–64°F)

Direct sunlight

Brassica oleracea Gongylodes Group

Kohl rabi

Kohl rabi is grown for its nutritious, globelike, swollen stem. There are green- and purple-skinned forms, both of which grow to 60cm (24in). Kohl rabi thrives in hot, dry conditions, and at the height of summer the stems will be ready to harvest eight weeks from sowing.

Sowing

Sow seed thinly in drills 2cm (¾in) deep and 30cm (12in) apart, in a well-prepared, finely sifted seedbed. Sow the quicker-maturing, green-skinned types from mid-spring to mid-summer, and the hardier, purple-skinned types from mid- to late summer.

Cultivation

When the first 'true' leaf develops, thin seedlings to 20cm (8in) apart.

Harvesting

The swollen stems are ready when they are 8–10cm (3–4in) across. The newer cultivars can grow much larger, because they remain tender. Cut through the taproot just below the swollen stem.

H 60m (24in)
S 90cm (36in)

20–25°C
(68–78°F)

Direct sunlight

Foeniculum vulgare Azoricum Group

Florence fennel

Florence fennel is grown for its succulent bulb, which has a distinctive aniseed flavour, the edible part being the swollen bases of its decorative, feathery leaves.

It prefers well-drained but moisture-retentive, fertile soil which has had plenty of organic matter incorporated 6–8 weeks before planting. The bulbs are ready to harvest about 14 weeks after sowing.

Sowing

Sow seed in modules under protection from early spring onwards. Set in a temperature of 16°C (61°F) if growing in a greenhouse; seeds germinated in a polytunnel require 12–14°C (54–57°F), or 10°C (50°F) in a cold frame.

Cultivation

About six weeks after sowing, harden off the seedlings in a cold frame. Plant them out from early summer onwards, after two 'true' leaves have developed, in rows 30cm (12in) apart and with 40cm (16in) between plants. When the bulbs begin to swell, cover the lower half with soil to blanch them.

Harvesting

The bulbs will be ready to harvest from late summer onwards, when they are 10cm (4in) across. Cut them off at soil level and trim away the leaves. Fennel can withstand light frost only, and does not store well.

H 60m (24in)
S 90cm (36in)

16–18°C
(62–64°F)

Direct sunlight

Rheum x *hybridum*, syn. *R.* x *cultorum*

Rhubarb

Often regarded as a fruit, but technically a vegetable, this herbaceous perennial is grown for its edible leaf stalks, which can be used for desserts and jam-making from mid-spring onwards. Rhubarb, which matures to a height of 30cm (12in) can be grown in the same plot for many years, but the well-drained, fertile soil must be dug deeply and plenty of organic matter incorporated prior to planting.

Planting
In late autumn, early winter, or spring plant one-year-old crowns about 1m (3ft) apart, with the young shoots ('eyes') just above soil level. If they are planted too deeply, the eyes will rot away.

Cultivation
Mulch the crowns well, keep the soil moist, and provide generous amounts of a balanced fertilizer after harvesting. Cut off any flowering spikes as they emerge in the spring and summer, and remove any spindly, unwanted leaves as they occur.

Harvesting
Pick the rhubarb when the stalks are 30cm (12in) long and deep pink in colour. Grip each stalk as close to its base as possible and twist it gently away from the crown. Discard the leaves, because they are not edible.

H 30cm (12in)
S 90cm (36in)

16–18°C
(62–64°F)

Partial shade

Bulb and Root Vegetables

Allium cepa
Onions

The strong-flavoured bulbs of onions are invaluable in the kitchen for a wide range of dishes. They are grown as annual plants, with the brown- or yellow-skinned cultivars being the most popular with gardeners.

Onions have a long growing season, and for good skin quality and colour the bulbs need plenty of bright sunshine in the period just before harvesting. Onions prefer a well-drained, fertile soil which has been well dug.

Sowing
In early autumn or early spring, sow seed in furrows 1.5cm (½in) deep and about 30cm (12in) apart, with 2.5cm (1in) between the seeds.

Cultivation
Onions suffer from weed competition, and keeping the plants weed-free by hoeing between rows until they establish (this takes about six weeks) is critical.

Harvesting
Onions are ready for harvesting when the leaves turn yellow and the tops keel over. The process can be speeded up by bending over the tops by hand, but this must be done carefully or the bulb may be bruised and will start to rot when in store. Lift the bulbs gently with a garden fork and allow them to dry naturally before storing in a cool, dry, frost-free place.

H 60cm (24in)
S 20cm (8in)

16–18°C
(62–64°F)

Direct sunlight

Allium cepa
Spring (salad) onions

Also known as bunching onions or scallions, they are fast-growing and can be used as an intercrop between larger-growing varieties or between carrots as a companion plant.

Sowing
Sow in drills every three to four weeks from early spring to late summer. Space seeds about 3cm (1¼in) apart with 15cm (6in) between rows. There is no need to thin further.

Cultivation
Keep weed-free and water in dry conditions.

Harvesting
Ready in 8–10 weeks. As soon as they reach a reasonable size, pull alternate plants as needed.

H 60cm (24in)
S 20cm (8in)

16–18°C
(62–64°F)

Direct sunlight

Allium sativum

Garlic

This hardy vegetable, with its characteristic strong flavour that makes such a valuable contribution to both cooked dishes and salads, is far easier to grow than many gardeners realize. There are two distinct forms – one white and the other purple.

Garlic has a long growing period, but will survive outdoors throughout the winter if grown in a light, dry, well-drained soil. On wetter soils, the plants should be grown on ridges to improve drainage.

Sowing

Dig over the soil deeply before planting in autumn. Split the bulbs into individual 'cloves' and push these into the soil, so that the top (pointed end) of the clove is approximately 2.5cm (1in) below the soil surface. For maximum yields and even bulb development, plant the cloves in a square arrangement at a spacing of 18cm (7in).

Cultivation

As they develop, the bulbs will gradually work their way up to the surface of the soil.

Harvesting

The bulbs will be ready to harvest as soon as the leaves begin to turn from green to yellow. Lift the bulbs gently with a garden fork and allow them to dry naturally before storing in a cool, dry, frost-free place.

H 60cm (24in)
S 20cm (8in)

16–18°C
(62–64°F)

Direct sunlight

Allium cepa Aggregatum Group
Shallots

Shallots have a very distinctive flavour and are easy to grow, but need a longer time in the ground than onions.

Sowing
Sow seed indoors in early spring, then plant outside in late spring, 15cm (6in) apart with 23–30cm (9–12in) between rows. Plant sets in situ in late winter (traditionally the shortest day), with the tips just showing, 15cm (6in) apart with 23–30cm (9–12in) between rows.

Cultivation
It is important to keep the site weed-free. Mulch to retain moisture. Water and feed spring-sown onions until mid-summer, then water only if they start to wilt. Feed overwintered bulbs once in early spring, cover with fleece to protect from frost if bulbs start to lift from the soil.

Harvesting
Ready in 26 weeks. Lift when the leaves die down, leave to dry out, then store as for onions. Healthy bulbs can be saved for replanting the following season.

H 60cm (24in)
S 20cm (8in)

16–18°C
(62–64°F)

Direct sunlight

Beta vulgaris

Beetroot

This useful root vegetable is a biennial plant which is grown as an annual, and can be used at just about any time of year either fresh, stored, or pickled. Although the round beetroot is the most common, other shapes such as oval, flat, and oblong are also grown. There is also a wide variation in colour – red being the most popular, but golden forms such as 'Burpee's Golden' and white ones are available.

Sowing

Sow from mid-spring through late summer. Soak the seed in warm water for half an hour before sowing to promote rapid germination, then sow thinly in furrows 2cm (¾in) deep and 30cm (12in) apart.

Cultivation

When the seedlings are about 2.5cm (1in) high, thin them to 7.5–10cm (3–4in) apart for large beets, and 4–5cm (1½–2in) to produce small, round beets for pickling.

Harvesting

Harvesting usually runs from early summer to mid-autumn, although beetroot can be harvested at any stage of growth depending on the size of beetroots required. The plants are not fully hardy, however, and should all be lifted for storage by late autumn. Dig up the beetroots with a garden fork and twist off the leaves, then use immediately or store the roots in a box of moist sand in a cool, dry, frost-free place.

H 23cm (9in)
S 25cm (10in)

16–18°C
(62–64°F)

Partial shade

Brassica napus Napobrassica Group
Swedes

This cream- to purple-skinned vegetable is one of the hardiest of all root crops and is grown for its mild, sweet-tasting, yellow flesh. Good cultivars are 'York' and 'American Purple Tops'.

Swedes require similar soil conditions to turnips. The roots will be ready to harvest about 24 weeks after sowing.

Sowing
Sow seed thinly in furrows 2cm (¾in) deep and 40cm (16in) apart in a finely sifted, well-prepared seedbed, from late spring onwards.

Cultivation
The soil should not be allowed to dry out at any stage, or a large proportion of the crop will develop forked roots and the plants may bolt. When the seedlings are 2.5cm (1in) high, thin them to 7–10cm (3–4in) apart, and then thin again three weeks later to leave the plants 25cm (10in) apart.

Harvesting
Swedes are usually ready to harvest from early to mid-autumn onwards. Although they survive well outdoors through the winter, the low temperatures often give the flesh a fibrous or woody texture. It is therefore advisable to lift them and store indoors.

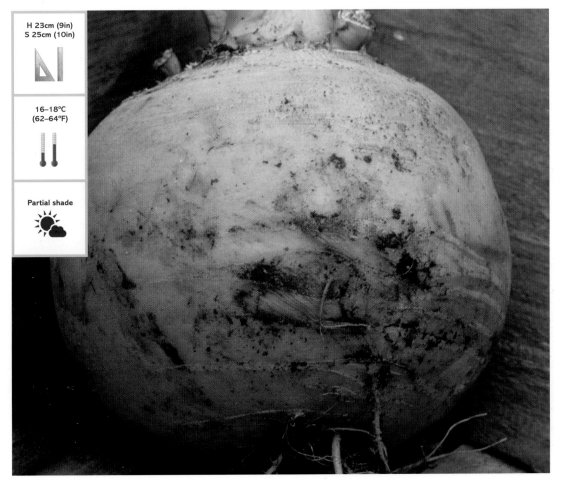

H 23cm (9in)
S 25cm (10in)

16–18°C
(62–64°F)

Partial shade

Brassica rapa Rapifera Group
Turnips

Often regarded as winter vegetables, turnips can be available throughout the year if a range of cultivars are grown in succession.

Turnips mature quickly and can easily be grown in a small container. They are mainly known as an ingredient of winter stews, but young turnips harvested when the size of golf balls are delicious.

Turnips prefer a light, fertile, well-drained but moisture-retentive soil which is high in nitrogen.

Sowing
Sow seed thinly in furrows 2cm (¾in) deep and 25–30cm (10–12in) apart in a finely sifted, well-prepared seedbed and subsequently at three-week intervals from late spring until mid- to late summer.

Cultivation
The soil should never be allowed to dry out, or much of the crop will develop forked roots and the plants may bolt. When seedlings are no higher than 2.5cm (1in), thin to 10cm (4in) apart for early cultivars, 15cm (6in) for later, hardy cultivars.

Harvesting
Turnips will be ready to harvest from early to mid-autumn, but must be lifted by mid-winter.

H 30–60cm
(12–24in)

16–18°C
(62–64°F)

Partial shade

Daucus carota

Carrots

Carrots are one of the most versatile of vegetables. You can grow them in one form or another throughout the year, from the young pencil carrots that are ready in early summer to the semi-mature roots that can be lifted later in the summer and through the autumn. These are followed by the mature vegetables that are stored for use over the winter. Carrots must have a deep and fertile soil that is able to hold plenty of moisture. In particular, you need to grow the early varieties quickly if they are to be tender and tasty. Never grow carrots on land that has just had compost or manure dug in, as they usually produce divided roots. For the earliest crops of tender, young carrots, broadcast the seed, rather than sow it in rows, during early spring.

Cultivation
Thin the seedlings to 4–7cm (1½–2¾in) apart for medium-sized carrots, 7–10cm (2¾–4in) for larger carrots suitable for storing through the winter. Thinning is best done in the evening or in cool, dull conditions to deter carrot rust fly. Hoe between the rows until foliage shades the soil and reduces weeds.

Harvesting
Early carrots can be eased out with a fork and then pulled by hand. Dig up maincrop carrots with a fork for immediate use, freezing or storing. Twist off and then discard the foliage.

H 30cm (12in)
S 8cm (3in)

16–18°C
(62–64°F)

Direct sunlight

Helianthus tuberosus
Jerusalem artichokes

Grown for its edible root, the hardy Jerusalem artichoke is also used to help clear rough ground. A vigorous perennial and relative of the sunflower, it can grow to a height of 3m (10ft), although the cultivar 'Dwarf Sunray' will reach only about 2m (6ft).

Sowing
Plant purchased tubers in spring, 10–15cm (4–6in) deep, in deeply cultivated soil. Plant in rows 60cm (24in) apart, with 30cm (12in) between the tubers. Large tubers can be divided up so that each piece has a separate shoot, and the sections planted individually.

Cultivation
When the plants are 30cm (12in) high, mound up the soil 15cm (6in) high around the base to keep the plants stable. In summer, cut the stems down to 1.5m (5ft) to encourage tuber formation. In dry weather, irrigate to keep the tubers swelling.

Harvesting
The tubers are ready from mid-autumn onwards and should be dug up with a garden fork. In well-drained soils, the tubers can be overwintered in the growing site. When harvesting, remove all parts of the tubers from the soil, or they will resprout next season.

H 2–3m
(6–10ft)

16–18°C
(62–64°F)

Direct sunlight

Pastinaca sativa

Parsnips

These winter vegetables have a very distinctive flavour and are hardy enough to overwinter in the soil. Parsnips prefer a deep, stone-free, well-drained, fertile soil, but on shallow soils shorter-rooted cultivars can be used.

Sowing

Sow seed thinly in furrows 1.5cm (½in) deep and 30cm (12in) apart, in early spring. Fresh seed gives the best results.

Cultivation

When the seedlings are about 2.5cm (1in) high, thin them to 7–10cm (2¾–4in) apart to produce large roots suitable for overwintering.

Harvesting

The roots will be ready to be lifted from mid-autumn onwards. Dig them up with a fork.

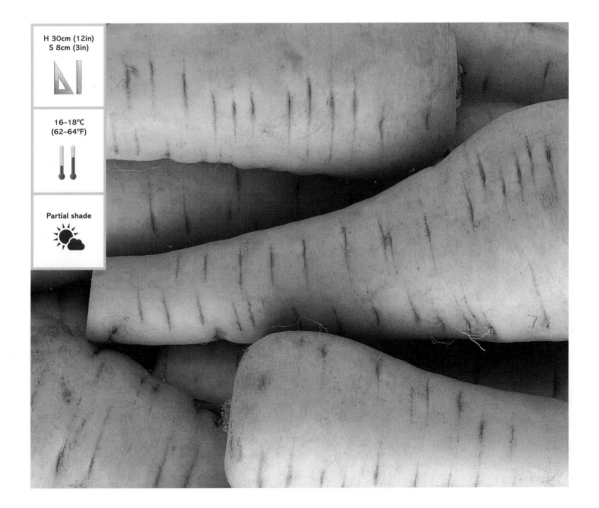

H 30cm (12in)
S 8cm (3in)

16–18°C
(62–64°F)

Partial shade

Raphanus sativus
Radish

One of the easiest of all vegetables to grow, radishes are the best way to introduce children to gardening. They germinate easily and mature quickly, in about a month. Gardeners with large vegetable gardens often use them as a marker crop between rows of vegetables that take longer to germinate and for the adventurous there are a number of winter-maturing radishes and the giant Japanese mooli radishes.

Sowing
Sow seed thinly in furrows 13 mm (½in) deep and about 15cm (6in) apart. For a continuous supply, sow seed at 10-day intervals from early spring through early autumn. The seed will keep for up to 10 years if kept cool and stored in an airtight container.

Cultivation
Radishes produce poor plants if overcrowded, and ideally they should be about 3cm (1in) apart. Watering is essential: drought will make the roots woody or encourage the plants to bolt.

Harvesting
Radishes are ready to harvest when the roots are about 3cm (1in) across at their widest point. Grip the plant firmly by its leaves and pull gently. If the soil is dry, water the plants the day before harvesting so that they will pull out of the ground easily.

H 30cm (12in)
S 8cm (3in)

16–18°C
(62–64°F)

Partial shade

Scorzonera hispanica
Black salsify

This hardy, perennial plant is, like carrots, usually grown as an annual for its thick, fleshy roots. These are about 20cm (8in) long and have a shiny, black skin – and a distinctive flavour when cooked. The young shoots (chards) and flower buds are also edible. It needs to have a deep, fertile soil in order to do well and produce a good crop.

Sowing
Sow seed thinly in furrows ½in (1 cm) deep and 20cm (8in) apart, in spring.

Cultivation
Thin the seedlings to 10cm (4in) apart soon after

germination. In order to achieve maximum growth, keep the plants weed-free and make sure they are well watered.

Harvesting
The roots will be ready to harvest from late autumn onwards. In mild areas, the roots can be lifted and used immediately, but in colder areas they should be lifted and stored in boxes of sand before winter weather sets in.

Roots that are over-wintered in the ground can be covered with straw in early spring. Young shoots will emerge through the straw, and these (and the flower buds) can be harvested when they are about 10cm (4in) high.

H 60cm (24in)
S 30cm (12in)

16–18°C
(62–64°F)

Direct sunlight

Solanum tuberosum
Potato

This versatile vegetable is divided into three main groups: earlies (quicker-growing cultivars); maincrop (slower-growing cultivars, producing heavier crops); and mid-season, which mature between the other two. Most early-season potatoes are ready to harvest from early summer onwards, and do not store well. Maincrop potatoes are available from mid-summer through into winter and can be stored.

Sowing
'Seed' is the term used for young potato tubers which are planted to produce the next crop. Purchase good-quality 'seed' potatoes in late winter and arrange the tubers in shallow trays to chit in early spring.

Cultivation
In most areas, planting can commence from mid-spring onwards for earlies, finishing with the last of the maincrop tubers by early to mid-summer. Plant the tubers 40cm (16in) apart, in rows 60cm (2ft) apart.

Harvesting
Early potatoes are ready for lifting when the flowers start to open. To harvest, use a garden fork to dig under the ridge of earth and ease the tubers from the soil to avoid 'stabbing' them.

Tragopogon porrifolius
Salsify

A hardy biennial plant, salsify is usually grown for its cream-white, fleshy roots, although its shoots are also edible. Because of its delicious flavour, it is often called the 'vegetable oyster'.

In order to achieve maximum growth, salsify requires a deep, well-drained fertile soil.

Sowing
Sow seed in furrows 1cm (½in) deep and 15cm (6in) apart, in spring. Fresh seed gives the best results, since salsify seed loses viability very quickly.

Cultivation
Thin the seedlings to 10cm (4in) apart soon after germination. To encourage rapid growth, keep the plants weed-free and well watered.

Harvesting
The roots will be ready to harvest from late autumn onwards. In mild areas, the roots can be lifted and used as required, but in colder areas the roots should be lifted and stored in boxes of sand (see opposite) before winter frost sets in.

H 30cm (12in)
S 8cm (3in)

16–18°C
(62–64°F)

Partial shade

H 60cm (24in)
S 30cm (12in)

16–18°C
(62–64°F)

Direct sunlight

Glossary

Annual A plant that lives for one year only. Most vegetables are annuals.

Biennial A plant which lasts for two years. The first season is a leaf and shoot growing phase, during which energy is stored for the second season's flowering. Biennial vegetables are cropped after the first year. Examples include parsnips and carrots.
Bolting 'Running to seed' or flowering before you want. In many cases this will ruin the vegetable you are trying to grow.

Catch cropping Sometimes one vegetable crop comes to an end a couple of months before you are ready to plant the next crop on that part of ground. Catch cropping is when you sow a quick maturing crop in this vacant gap.
Chitting Germinating seed before sowing. This is always done for potatoes, and may also be done for other seeds, such as sweetcorn, by placing them in a damp, warm place.

Green manure A crop grown specifically for digging back into the soil. These may be grown to protect the ground between crops, to stop nutrients leaking away, or to provide green matter and nitrogen ready for the next crops.

Half-hardy Plants unable to survive the winter without protection. Examples include runner beans and sweetcorn.
Harden off The gradual acclimatization of seedlings grown indoors or in greenhouses to outside conditions, before transplanting. This is often done in a cold frame which is gradually opened more and more each day to let in more 'cold' air.
Hardy Plants able to survive the winter without protection. Examples of hardy vegetables include brussels sprouts and broccoli.

Intercropping Growing small crops in the spaces alongside larger plants, or alongside plants which are so slow growing that before they reach maturity the smaller crop will have been harvested.

Mulch A layer of material placed over the ground, for the purposes of feeding the soil, conserving moisture, stopping weeds germinating, keeping the soil warm or protecting from heavy rain.

Offset A small, complete plant produced by many bulbous plants. It can be easily removed from the original bulb and planted on to produce another plant.

Perennial Plants that live for more than two years. Examples of vegetables that are left in the same spot for many years include rhubarb and asparagus.
Pricking out Moving tiny seedlings from pots or trays into new pots, to give them more room.

Seed bed A specific bed where seeds are sown for germination and development into small seedlings with the intention that they will later be transplanted to their final growing position.

Transplanting Taking seedlings from a seed bed or container and planting them where they will grow to maturity. Brassicas are usually transplanted (because they need more room when they grow to maturity than they do when just germinating). Root crops generally grow poorly after transplanting. In general, water the seedlings the day before you lift them, and water again after they have been planted in their new position.
True leaves When a seed germinates a pair of leaves is produced. The set of leaves to appear after these are the 'true leaves'. They look much more like smaller versions of the leaves of the mature plant.
Tuber The swollen part of a plant underground that stores energy. Potatoes are tubers.

Index